GETTYSBURG BATTLEFIELD
TODAY
PENNSYLVANIA RAILROAD

Gettysburg

PREVIOUS EDITION

EDITOR
Ben Nussbaum

CHIEF CONTENT OFFICER
June Kikuchi

SENIOR ART DIRECTOR/
DESIGN MANAGER
Véronique Bos

ART DIRECTOR
Cindy Kassebaum

CURRENT EDITION

MANAGING EDITOR
Gretchen Bacon

DESIGN AND PRODUCTION
MANAGER
David Fisk

DESIGNER
Christopher Morrison

EDITORIAL ASSISTANT, BOOKS
Christa Oestreich

ISBN 978-1-49710-326-9

Library of Congress Control Number:
2021953519

To learn more about the other great books from
Fox Chapel Publishing, or to find a retailer near
you, call toll-free 800-457-9112 or visit us at
www.FoxChapelPublishing.com.

We are always looking for talented authors. To
submit an idea, please send a brief inquiry to
acquisitions@foxchapelpublishing.com.

Printed in China
First Printing

Gettysburg

The Battle of Gettysburg

For three days in July of 1863, the fate of the Union hung in the balance as Confederates and Federals fought in the hills, fields and streets of Gettysburg.

By Peter C. Luebke

PUBLISHED BY CURRIER & IVES,

THE BATT

This terrific and bloody conflict between the gallant Army under General Lee, was commenced on Wednesday July plete rout & dispersion of the Rebel Army. A Nations th

The town of Gettysburg was unimportant.

The Confederate Army had crossed the Potomac searching for much-needed supplies, to give war-ravaged Virginia a respite and to possibly threaten Washington, Baltimore or Philadelphia. Gen. Robert E. Lee hoped that a major victory would soften Northern support for the war, possibly bringing the fighting to an end.

By late June, Lee's army had divided to attack different cities in resource-rich Pennsylvania. When Lee realized that the Union Army was in close pursuit, he ordered his soldiers to regroup in anticipation of a major battle.

A skirmish in Gettysburg on June 30 led to intense fighting on July 1. The cry for reinforcements went out. The Confederate and Union Armies had found each other. Soldiers poured into the area. The fight that turned the tide of the war had begun.

162 NASSAU ST. NEW YORK.

OF GETTYSBURG, Pᴬ JULY 3ᴰ 1863.

Potomac", commanded by their great General George G. Meade, and the hosts of the rebel "Army of the East"
d ended on Friday the 3ʳᵈ at 5 O'Clock P. M. — The decisive Battle was fought on Friday, ending in the com-
and undying fame ever crown the Arms of the heroic soldiers, who fought with such unflinching bravery
this long and desperate fight.

J uly 1, 1863, found Lee and Union Gen. George G. Meade's armies spread out across Maryland and central Pennsylvania. Since crossing into Pennsylvania, Lee's Army of Northern Virginia had been on a grand raid, confiscating supplies and sending them southward. Meade, newly in command of the Army of the Potomac, pursued the Confederates but firm knowledge of their whereabouts remained elusive. Likewise, Lee had only a foggy notion regarding the disposition of the Union troops, as the bulk of Lee's cavalry remained out of touch.

Neither Lee nor Meade planned on fighting a major battle at Gettysburg, but both knew that a major confrontation was pending.

Early on the morning of July 1, a division of Confederates led by Henry Heth, of Lt. Gen. A. P. Hill's 3rd Corps, embarked on an expedition to Gettysburg. They had been in the area the day before and observed troops in the crossroads town and sought to drive them off. As the Confederates marched along Chambersburg Pike, they encountered Union troops posted west of Gettysburg along ridges that made excellent defensive positions. The troops were Brig. Gen. John Buford's cavalry. Buford aimed to delay the Confederate advance into town, allowing the nearby 1st Corps led by John F. Reynolds time to concentrate his unit in support. The first shots of what would be a three-day battle were fired around 7 a.m. on July 1, a Wednesday, with the first action involving several thousand men.

For most of the morning, the Union troops held their position as Hill hurried more Confederates to the scene. Ultimately the Federals fell back to McPherson's Ridge, where they repulsed Confederate infantry attacks. Elements of Lt. Gen. Richard S. Ewell's 2nd Corps of Lee's army, situated north of Gettysburg, turned south.

TOM EISHEN / GETTYSBURGPHOTOGRAPHS.COM

Cemetery Hill, including a monument to Maj. Gen. Oliver Howard.

Troops heading to the reserve line streamed through Gettysburg, pouring through the streets to the astonishment of the townspeople, who had not expected a pitched battle on their doorsteps.

Reynolds, although killed on the field of battle hours after the first shots were fired, had bought time for the Army of the Potomac to begin to concentrate on the field. Maj. Gen. Oliver Otis Howard arrived and began to bring his 11th Corps to the battle. Howard slotted his troops in to the right flank of Reynolds' men so that the Union line curved from the west to the north edge of Gettysburg. Prudently, Howard also established a reserve position along Cemetery Ridge to the south of the town.

The crisis for the Union line began around 2:30 p.m. Ewell's divisions had arrived on the field in nearly the perfect place. One slammed into the Union center near Oak Ridge while the other pressed the Union right flank north of Gettysburg. The Union right flank collapsed, and the entire line north of Gettysburg unraveled. Troops heading to the reserve line streamed through Gettysburg, pouring into the streets to the astonishment of the townspeople, who had not expected a pitched battle on their doorsteps. Although Lee ordered Ewell to attack Cemetery Hill late in the day, Ewell's men were too tired from marching and fighting to capitalize on the opportunity.

Lee and his troops had won a victory, but the Union army occupied a strong position. The Union line resembled a fishhook, with the hook curving around from Culp's Hill and the shank stretching down along Cemetery Ridge toward Little Round Top and Big Round Top. The Union position forced Lee to place his men on the facing Seminary Ridge. Lee's line was longer than Meade's; during the battle the next day, Meade could more easily move men to meet threats as there was a shorter distance for them to travel.

On the second day of the battle, Lee intended to launch two divisions of Gen. James Longstreet's 1st Corps against the Union left flank. If Longstreet could shatter the Union position there, he could roll up the Army of the Potomac. Meanwhile, Ewell's 2nd Corps, on the right flank of the Army of the Potomac, would attack the troops occupying Culp's Hill in an effort to prevent them from reinforcing the Union left. Lee also ordered one division of Hill's 3rd Corps to participate.

Lee's plan had several problems. First, Longstreet's men would need to get into position before the attack could begin. On the evening of July 1, they were still several miles from the battlefield. Second, the time that Longstreet took to get his men into position would allow the Army of the Potomac to strengthen its left. The Union's 3rd Corps under Maj. Gen. Daniel Sickles spent the morning occupying the Peach Orchard, high ground between the Confederate forces and the Union troops waiting on Cemetery Ridge.

Longstreet's men spent the morning and early afternoon marching to and fro in an effort to get into position. Lee wanted Longstreet to conceal his movements from the enemy, so Longstreet's troops marched on routes that were not the most direct in an attempt to avoid being spotted by the Union army. Longstreet also had to modify his attack plan; he had expected to hit the Union flank, but one of his divisions would now have to make a frontal assault on the Peach Orchard. Finally, around 4 p.m., Longstreet's men stood ready to attack. Union forces had spent the day preparing for the inevitable Confederate assault, fortifying their position.

The fighting began when John Bell Hood's division of Longstreet's corps, farthest on the Confederate right, advanced on the Union line. Hood's men marched toward Little Round Top on the extreme Union left. Earlier in the day, Union Brig. Gen. Gouverneur K. Warren had noticed that this key position needed to be protected. The soldiers arrived just in time and held off the Confederate advance. During the course of the fighting, Col. Joshua L. Chamberlain of the 20th Maine Infantry Regiment famously ordered a bayonet charge that blunted the initial Confederate attack. Chamberlain would later be awarded the Medal of Honor for his heroics at Gettysburg. Although it appeared for a short time that the Confederates would turn the Union flank at Little Round Top, the success of the defenders enabled Meade to send reinforcements to bolster the position.

As the situation began to stabilize at the far left of the line, Sickles' position at the Peach Orchard began to crumble, throwing the Army of the Potomac into a crisis. In posting his men there, Sickles had occupied a position advanced from the main Union line, creating a protrusion vulnerable to attacks from several directions.

Meade had reinforced the position, but it remained dangerously exposed. Thus, as Hood's division pressed hard against Little Round Top and nearby Devil's Den, Longstreet ordered in Lafayette McLaws' division to battle the remaining Union troops at the Peach Orchard. McLaws first cleared Union troops from the Wheatfield, then slammed into the flank of the line at the Peach Orchard. Overwhelmed, the Federals fell back. A gaping hole now existed in the Union lines between the troops posted along Cemetery Ridge and those holding Little Round Top.

Sickles' corps had collapsed, and Sickles himself was sent to the rear with a wound that necessitated the amputation of one of his legs. Now the Confederates had to hold on to their hard won gains and continue their advance. Union Gen. Winfield Scott Hancock brought his 2nd Corps into action. His men blunted the Confederate advance before throwing them back, which enabled Meade to bring reinforcements into position and plug the gap along Cemetery Ridge. As the day turned to dusk, the Union Army had staved off disaster and repulsed the Confederate threat to its left flank.

As the situation began to stabilize at the far left of the line, Sickles' position at the Peach Orchard began to crumble, throwing the Army of the Potomac into a crisis.

Culp's Hill

As the fighting petered out on the Union left, Ewell's men around Culp's Hill and Cemetery Hill attacked. At around 7 p.m., Ewell ordered his entire 2nd Corps to advance. His men faced a difficult situation, as the Union troops on Culp's Hill had spent the day entrenching and fortifying their position. Although weakened because they had sent reinforcements to the left during the day, the troops of the 12th Corps still on the hill held off Ewell's men. Some Union defenses on Culp's Hill fell, and Jubal A. Early's division managed to break a portion of the lines on Cemetery Hill. This penetration turned out to be brief as the Confederates pulled back in the face of a counterattack. Meade had narrowly staved off disaster.

While the collapse of Sickles' 3rd Corps had almost proved fatal, the timely arrival of Hancock's men preserved the line. The diminished force on Culp's Hill and Cemetery Hill had also held off the Confederate attackers. Lee, considering his options, determined to continue the fight on the third day. From his perspective, it appeared as if he had almost crushed his opponent: His men had dismantled the Union 3rd Corps at the Peach Orchard and nearly prevailed at Little Round Top. He knew he had grievously wounded Meade's army. While most men slept on the field, Maj. Gen. George Pickett's division of Longstreet's corps arrived.

The second day was Gettysburg's bloodiest with over 20,000 casualties — men killed, wounded or missing.

Fighting on Friday, July 3 began at Culp's Hill, where Confederate troops still occupied portions of the lines they had captured the night before. Although heavy fighting raged all morning long, Ewell's men could gain no ground.

As the fighting at Culp's Hill wound down on that morning, Longstreet prepared for the grand assault of the day. Lee had nearly beaten the Army of the Potomac the previous day and understood that Meade had stripped his center of troops to reinforce the left flank. He reasoned that an assault on a weakened Union center might prevail. The attack known to posterity as Pickett's Charge included men from George Pickett's fresh division as well as brigades from J. Johnston Pettigrew and Isaac Trimble's divisions that had not been heavily engaged on July 2. More than 100 artillery pieces aligned atop Seminary Ridge began a preparatory bombardment at about 1 p.m., with the hopes that the barrage would weaken the Union defenders. Due to the difficulty of adjusting aim amid the clouds of smoke, much of the Confederate fire sailed over the heads of the Union troops. The Federals also were sheltered on the reverse of the slope of Cemetery Ridge, largely protecting them from the shelling.

With artillery ammunition dwindling and the Union batteries that had crowned Cemetery Ridge nowhere to be seen, the Confederate infantry stepped off to begin its advance. Nearly 12,000 Confederate infantry stood ready. Regimental flags waved in the breeze as the charge began, with the rank and file moving forward in good order. They faced nearly three-quarters of a mile of open field before they reached the Union line. At the center of that line stood a small cluster of trees, known to history as the Copse of Trees, that the Confederates would head toward.

The Union artillery, back in position after the Confederate cannonade, opened fire on the Confederate infantry. Artillery shells cut large swaths through the ranks of gray as the Confederates deliberately advanced across the field. The Union infantry of the 2nd Corps under Winfield Scott Hancock readied their muskets.

When the Confederate infantry closed to within 400 feet, the Union infantry let loose a devastating volley. While the center of the Confederate line continued forward, the left flank began to crumble. Seeing an opportunity, Union infantry swung down on it like a hinge, pouring enfilading fire into the column and inflicting grievous casualties. Hancock ordered the Vermont brigade under his command to swing down on the right of the Confederate line.

As the flanks encountered trouble, the center of the Confederate line, spearheaded by the Virginians of Pickett's division, crashed into the Union line near the Copse of Trees. Union artillery blasted canister into the waves of infantry, but the Confederates stormed over the guns. Brig. Gen. Lewis Armistead rallied his men by brandishing his hat upon his sword.

Union infantry beat back the penetration and halted this last Confederate advance. Despite their success, Pickett's men who had reached the Union line amid the slaughter of their brethren had little chance of success. With no support on the way, they had no way to capitalize on the breach they created.

Lee's gamble to crack the Union center had failed. Confederate losses in the charge were catastrophic, with around 7,000 casualties, compared to just 1,500 for the Union. Meade and the Army of the Potomac had won, bringing a halt to Lee's invasion of the North. Ⓖ

With artillery ammunition dwindling and the Union batteries that had crowned Cemetery Ridge nowhere to be seen, the Confederate infantry stepped off to begin its advance. Nearly 12,000 Confederate infantry stood ready.

Cemetery Ridge, looking toward the fields where Pickett's Charge occurred.

Robert E. Lee

Commander of the Army of Northern Virginia

Robert E. Lee was the principal military figure of the South during most of the Civil War. Even before the war he was one of the finest soldiers of his generation, coming second in his class at West Point, distinguishing himself as an aide to Gen. Winfield Scott in the Mexican-American War and serving as Superintendent of West Point. A member of one of Virginia's most prominent families — the son of one of the Revolution's heroes, Henry "Light-Horse Harry" Lee, and the husband of George Washington's great-granddaughter — there was little doubt whose side Lee would choose in 1861. However, he did not promote the cause of secession and waited until his own state voted for it before taking up arms against the Union. President Abraham Lincoln had even asked Lee to command the forces of the North.

In keeping with the military thinking of his day, Lee subscribed to the doctrine of the offensive and excelled at maneuver. His plan for winning the war relied on a series of set-piece battle victories against Northern troops as a prelude to expelling Union forces from the South and then suing for peace with a chastened North. Lee's superior generalship and zealous troops achieved several important victories against the North on Southern soil. As the war went on, it became less popular in the North than in the South, giving Lee hope that his strategy might work.

Yet Lee had begun the war with a mixed reputation. Some people saw him as timid and hesitant; a few even called him Granny Lee. He put an end to that with his audacious attacks in the Seven Days Battle in the summer of 1862, followed by his victory at the Second Battle of Bull Run. But audacity would get the better of him. Lee decided to extend his victories farther north by invading Maryland and later Pennsylvania. This resulted in critical defeats at Antietam and Gettysburg. The first showed the South could lose; the second that the North might win.

Gettysburg turned the tide in the Civil War. From then on, Lee would fight a defensive campaign against better equipped and ably led Northern forces. All his talents as an operational commander could not make up for the strategic liabilities his side faced: a dwindling supply of troops and provisions and worsening morale on the Southern homefront.

Following the surrender he signed at Appomattox Court House on April 9, 1865, Lee served as the president of Washington College until his death in 1870, at which time the college changed its name to Washington and Lee University in his honor. Posterity has remembered him for his principal traits of character: his sense of duty, his self-discipline, his perfectionism, his loyalty and his bearing. He was an elegant, dignified, even gallant figure, much beloved by his soldiers.

— *Kenneth Weisbrode*

George G. Meade was born in Spain to American parents and came to the United States when he was 13, shortly after his father's death. He entered West Point, trained in artillery and engineering, but left the army in 1836 to work as a civilian engineer. He returned to the military six years later to improve his finances.

Meade served in the Mexican-American War and then in a series of engineering, surveying and infrastructure projects on the Great Lakes and throughout the South. He developed a particular expertise in the construction of lighthouses. Soon after the outbreak of the Civil War, he was promoted to brigadier general in command of Pennsylvania reservists. With the Army of the Potomac, his brigade fought admirably at Bull Run, in the Seven Days Battle, and at Antietam, Fredericksburg and Chancellorsville. He repeatedly impressed his commanders with his mastery of terrain and combat effectiveness. His men were also noted for the occasional act of heroism, as when, for example, they covered retreating Northern lines during the Second Battle of Bull Run by holding their position on Henry House Hill.

Meade's reputation for competence and bravery brought him notice. Gen. George McClellan and Gen. Joseph Hooker thought highly of him and saw to his promotion. By the fall of 1862 he was a major general serving under Hooker and had even replaced a wounded Hooker at Antietam. Meade would replace Hooker again on the eve of Gettysburg. After a dismal performance at Chancellorsville and disagreements over subsequent plans, Hooker abruptly resigned. Unlike him, Meade was not flamboyant or reckless. He was known for his workmanlike discipline mixed with a bold streak and impressive coolness under fire. This was a rare combination in a commander; it spoke to his toughness but also his determination, sometimes against tremendous pressure, to stay put when he did not feel a Confederate assault would succeed.

He was also known for a difficult, cold, terse and sometimes brutal manner. And yet, he once wrote that the North should treat the South "like the afflicted parent who is compelled to chastise the erring child, and who performs the duty with a sad heart."

His talents served him well at times, others less so. At Gettysburg he failed to stop Lee's defeated troops from escaping back to the South, to President Abraham Lincoln's great consternation. Although Gettysburg was a great victory for Meade, this decision is the reason usually given for him being less celebrated than other commanders.

Meade served out most of the remainder of the war alongside Gen. Ulysses S. Grant. The relationship between the two was difficult on account of the restrictions placed on Meade's autonomy and because the two had very different concepts of the war. On balance, however, the two worked successfully together. During this time Meade commanded troops at the Battles of the Wilderness, Spotsylvania, Cold Harbor and Petersburg, as well as many smaller battles.

After the war, Meade's army service continued, including a term as Reconstruction governor of Atlanta. Subsequently he spent the remainder of his years in Philadelphia.

— Kenneth Weisbrode

George G. Meade
Commander of the Army of the Potomac

THE BLUE and

THE ARMY OF THE POTOMAC

COMMANDER:
Gen. George G. Meade oversaw seven infantry corps and a cavalry corps.

STRENGTH: 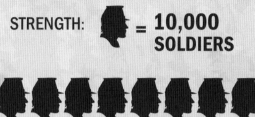 = **10,000 SOLDIERS**

= **94,000**

I CORPS: Maj. Gen. John F. Reynolds led the 1st Corps, which fought primarily on the first day of the battle. It also occupied Cemetery Ridge at the north of the Union line on the second and third days of the battle.

 II CORPS: Maj. Gen. Winfield Scott Hancock led the 2nd Corps, which occupied the center of the Union line on the second and third days of the battle.

III CORPS: Maj. Gen. Daniel E. Sickles led the 3rd Corps, which fought at the south end of the Union line in the Peach Orchard, the Wheatfield and Devil's Den.

 V CORPS: Maj. Gen. George Sykes led the 5th Corps, which fought at the extreme south end of the Union line at Little Round Top on the second day of the battle.

VI CORPS: Maj. Gen. John Sedgwick led the 6th Corps, which arrived on the battlefield late on the second day of the battle. It bolstered the Union position at Little Round Top but saw little action.

XI CORPS: Maj. Gen. Oliver Otis Howard led the 11th Corps, which fought north of Gettysburg on the first day and occupied positions on Cemetery Ridge on the second and third days of the battle.

 XII CORPS: Maj. Gen. Henry Slocum commanded the 12th Corps, which occupied Culp's Hill on the second and third days of the battle.

CAVALRY CORPS: Maj. Gen. Alfred Pleasonton led the Cavalry Corps of the Army of the Potomac. Cavalry unites were instrumental in delaying the Confederate advance on the first day and fought two battles against Confederate cavalry on the third day, both at a distance from the main battlefield.

 ARTILLERY RESERVE: Most of the Union artillery at Gettysburg (and all of the artillery on the Confederate side) was distributed amongst the various corps. However, several batteries were kept as an artillery reserve to be deployed around the battlefield as needed. The artillery reserve was led by Brig. Gen. Robert Tyler.

UNION CASUALTIES

3,155 killed ➕ **14,529** wounded ➕ **5,365** missing & captured 🟰 **23,049** total

THE GRAY *at Gettysburg*

THE ARMY OF NORTHERN VIRGINIA

COMMANDER: Gen. Robert E. Lee led three infantry corps and a division of cavalry.

STRENGTH: = **10,000 SOLDIERS**

= **72,000**

I CORPS: Lt. Gen. James Longstreet commanded the 1st Army Corps that fought mostly on the second day of the battle around the Peach Orchard, the Wheatfield and Devil's Den. George E. Pickett's division was part of Longstreet's corps.

II CORPS: Lt. Gen. Richard S. Ewell led the 2nd Army Corps that fought north of Gettysburg on the first day of the battle and launched attacks against Cemetery Hill and Culp's Hill on the next two days of the battle.

III CORPS: Lt. Gen. Ambrose Powell Hill led the 3rd Army Corps that was involved in the first skirmishes on the first day of the battle, west of the town of Gettysburg. Hill's men occupied the center of Lee's line on the second day and participated in Pickett's Charge on the third day.

CAVALRY CORPS: Maj. Gen. J.E.B. Stuart commanded the Cavalry Division of the Army of Northern Virginia. Absent for most of the battle, Stuart's division fought on the third day.

WOUNDED LEADERS

Of the 120 generals present at Gettysburg, nine were killed or mortally wounded.

TROOP ATTRITION
AT GETTYSBURG

At Gettysburg some regiments had almost their full strength of 1,000 men; others had only a few hundred men due to attrition. Some entire brigades, composed of multiple regiments, had fewer men than the paper strength of a single regiment.

CONFEDERATE CASUALTIES

3,903 killed **+** **18,735** wounded **+** **5,425** missing & captured **=** **28,063** total

Sources: Civil War Trust; NPS.gov; WW II Memorial; The Civil War Dictionary; Regimental Losses in the American Civil War, 1861-1865

GETTYSBURG TIMELINE

Day 1 — July 1, 1863

Confederate Lt. Gen. Richard Ewell

Confederate forces under Lt. Gen. Richard Ewell arrive from the north and take position on Oak Hill as the bulk of the Union 1st and 11th Corps approach Gettysburg from the south.

1 AM   2 AM   3 AM   4 AM   5 AM   6 AM   7 AM   8 AM   9 AM   10 AM   11 AM   NOON

Union Gen. John Buford

First shot of the battle is fired. Advanced forces under Confederate Gen. Henry Heth skirmish with Union Gen. John Buford's men in the field west of town along the Chambersburg Pike.

The Confederate infantry advances in force and encounters Union infantry of the 1st Corps under Maj. Gen. John F. Reynolds. The Southerners are driven back but Reynolds is killed in the fighting.

Union Maj. Gen. John F. Reynolds

Day 2 — July 2, 1863

Confederate Lt. Gen. James Longstreet

After a long march, Confederate infantry of Lt. Gen. James Longstreet's 1st Corps move into position along Seminary Ridge. Southern artillery pounds the Union lines.

1 AM   2 AM   3 AM   4 AM   5 AM   6 AM   7 AM   8 AM   9 AM   10 AM   11 AM   NOON

MORNING: As Union Gen. George G. Meade brings up reinforcements, Lee determines to move his troops into position and drive in both ends of the Union line.

Union Gen. George G. Meade

AFTERNOON: Dissatisfied with his assigned position, Union Maj. Gen. Daniel Sickles advances his 3rd Corps to Emmitsburg Road, endangering the Union left flank.

Union Maj. Gen. Daniel Sickles

Day 3 — July 3, 1863

An uneasy lull falls over the field.

Confederate artillery opens fire all along the line. Union cannons fire in return. For almost two hours the earth rumbles.

1 AM   2 AM   3 AM   4 AM   5 AM   6 AM   7 AM   8 AM   9 AM   10 AM   11 AM   NOON

MORNING: Fighting erupts early in the day along the slopes of Culp's Hill. After hours of continuous fighting, the Confederates are driven back.

Culp's Hill

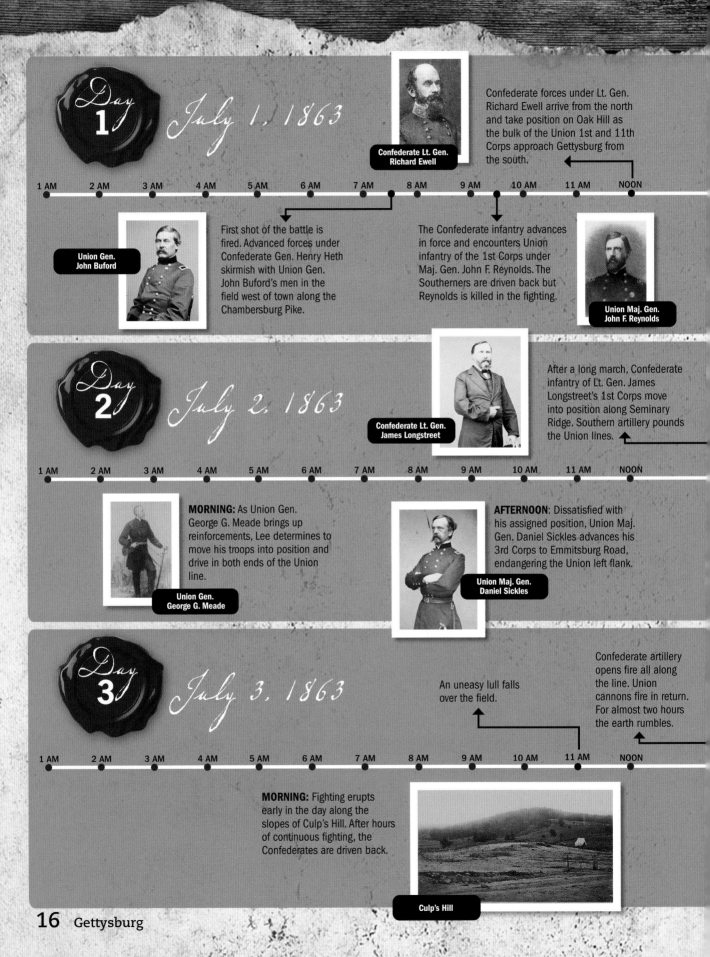

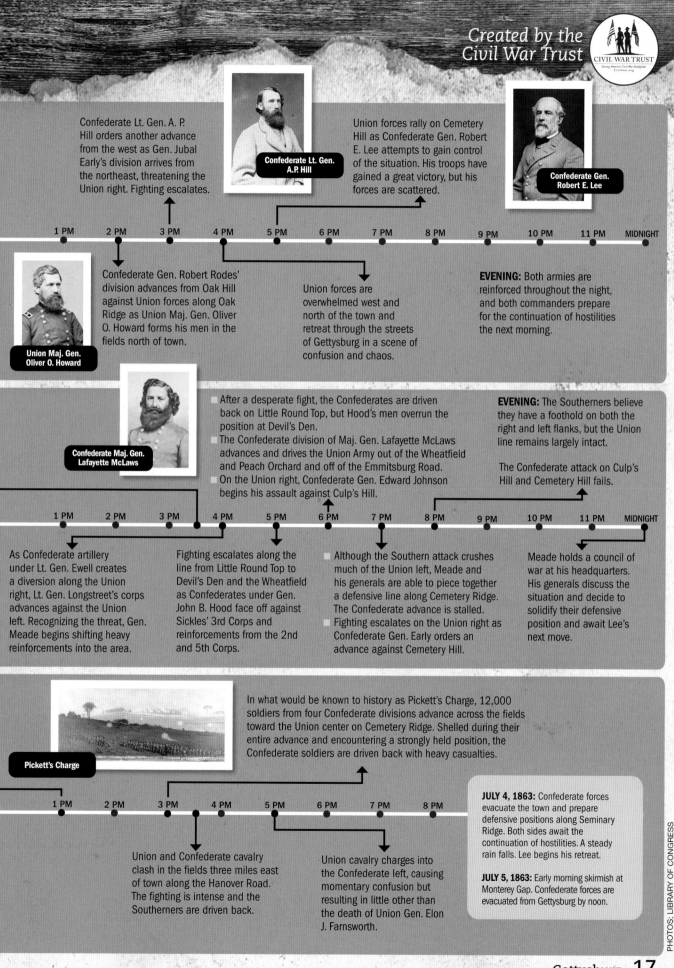

Confederate Lt. Gen. A. P. Hill orders another advance from the west as Gen. Jubal Early's division arrives from the northeast, threatening the Union right. Fighting escalates.

Confederate Lt. Gen. A.P. Hill

Union forces rally on Cemetery Hill as Confederate Gen. Robert E. Lee attempts to gain control of the situation. His troops have gained a great victory, but his forces are scattered.

Confederate Gen. Robert E. Lee

1 PM 2 PM 3 PM 4 PM 5 PM 6 PM 7 PM 8 PM 9 PM 10 PM 11 PM MIDNIGHT

Union Maj. Gen. Oliver O. Howard

Confederate Gen. Robert Rodes' division advances from Oak Hill against Union forces along Oak Ridge as Union Maj. Gen. Oliver O. Howard forms his men in the fields north of town.

Union forces are overwhelmed west and north of the town and retreat through the streets of Gettysburg in a scene of confusion and chaos.

EVENING: Both armies are reinforced throughout the night, and both commanders prepare for the continuation of hostilities the next morning.

Confederate Maj. Gen. Lafayette McLaws

☐ After a desperate fight, the Confederates are driven back on Little Round Top, but Hood's men overrun the position at Devil's Den.
☐ The Confederate division of Maj. Gen. Lafayette McLaws advances and drives the Union Army out of the Wheatfield and Peach Orchard and off of the Emmitsburg Road.
☐ On the Union right, Confederate Gen. Edward Johnson begins his assault against Culp's Hill.

EVENING: The Southerners believe they have a foothold on both the right and left flanks, but the Union line remains largely intact.

The Confederate attack on Culp's Hill and Cemetery Hill fails.

1 PM 2 PM 3 PM 4 PM 5 PM 6 PM 7 PM 8 PM 9 PM 10 PM 11 PM MIDNIGHT

As Confederate artillery under Lt. Gen. Ewell creates a diversion along the Union right, Lt. Gen. Longstreet's corps advances against the Union left. Recognizing the threat, Gen. Meade begins shifting heavy reinforcements into the area.

Fighting escalates along the line from Little Round Top to Devil's Den and the Wheatfield as Confederates under Gen. John B. Hood face off against Sickles' 3rd Corps and reinforcements from the 2nd and 5th Corps.

☐ Although the Southern attack crushes much of the Union left, Meade and his generals are able to piece together a defensive line along Cemetery Ridge. The Confederate advance is stalled.
☐ Fighting escalates on the Union right as Confederate Gen. Early orders an advance against Cemetery Hill.

Meade holds a council of war at his headquarters. His generals discuss the situation and decide to solidify their defensive position and await Lee's next move.

Pickett's Charge

In what would be known to history as Pickett's Charge, 12,000 soldiers from four Confederate divisions advance across the fields toward the Union center on Cemetery Ridge. Shelled during their entire advance and encountering a strongly held position, the Confederate soldiers are driven back with heavy casualties.

1 PM 2 PM 3 PM 4 PM 5 PM 6 PM 7 PM 8 PM

JULY 4, 1863: Confederate forces evacuate the town and prepare defensive positions along Seminary Ridge. Both sides await the continuation of hostilities. A steady rain falls. Lee begins his retreat.

JULY 5, 1863: Early morning skirmish at Monterey Gap. Confederate forces are evacuated from Gettysburg by noon.

Union and Confederate cavalry clash in the fields three miles east of town along the Hanover Road. The fighting is intense and the Southerners are driven back.

Union cavalry charges into the Confederate left, causing momentary confusion but resulting in little other than the death of Union Gen. Elon J. Farnsworth.

Lincoln's Gettysburg

Far from being a distant observer, President Lincoln shaped Gettysburg, followed the action closely, and forever changed the way we think of the battle.

By Brian Dirck
Photos from the Library of Congress

When Abraham Lincoln held his weekly cabinet meeting on June 23, 1863, Robert E. Lee's Army of Northern Virginia was marching northward, adding to the worries of a shockingly weary, prematurely aged president. "He looks more careworn even than usual," remarked the poet Walt Whitman, who saw Lincoln at about this time. "His face cut with deep lines, seams, and his complexion gray ... [a] curious looking man, very sad."

Lincoln and Gen. McClellan in Antietam, Maryland, in October 1862. The Battle at Antietam was a decisive Union victory, but Lincoln was unhappy with McClellan's slow pursuit of the wounded Confederate Army.

Lincoln had met with the commander of the Army of the Potomac, Joseph Hooker, that morning. Apparently the president did not like what he was hearing about Lee's march and Union prospects for ending it. When he joined the cabinet "his countenance was sad," according to Gideon Welles, the Secretary of the Navy.

Who is "The Man"?

No one, it seemed, was capable of leading the Army of the Potomac to victory. "We cannot help beating them, if we have the man," Lincoln believed. But "the man" proved elusive; it was this ongoing, frustrating search for a Union general who could win battles against the now-legendary Lee that would haunt Lincoln throughout the Gettysburg campaign.

At one time, Gen. George McClellan, the handsome "Young Napoleon" appointed by Lincoln to command the entire Union war effort in the fall of 1861, seemed to be that leader. "I can do it all," McClellan confidently assured the president. But on the battlefield he was timid (Lincoln caustically observed he suffered from the "slows") and indecisive. He also constantly badgered Lincoln for more men — despite nearly always outnumbering his Confederate foes — and found endless excuses for delay.

The general came from a wealthy family, was more than a little snobbish, and privately disparaged Lincoln as a "well-meaning baboon" and the "original gorilla." For his part, Lincoln tried to accommodate McClellan, but their relationship grew increasingly strained. "I beg to assure you that I have never written you, or spoken to you, in greater kindness of feeling than now," Lincoln wrote, "but you must act."

McClellan represented a vision of the war that fell considerably short of grand conquest. The war "should be conducted upon the highest principles known to Christian civilization," McClellan wrote to Lincoln, "it should not look to the subjugation of the people of any state. ...Neither

confiscation of property, political executions of persons, territorial organization of states or forcible abolition of slavery should be contemplated for a moment." On that last point, especially, McClellan was adamant: "a declaration of radical views, especially upon slavery, will rapidly disintegrate our present armies."

When McClellan allowed Lee's army to escape after the mauling it received at the Battle of Antietam in September 1862, Lincoln finally lost all patience. McClellan was sent packing. At the same time, Lincoln announced his intention to make emancipation a primary Union war aim, rejecting not just McClellan but the limited vision of the war that he represented. The president "has made a terrible mistake," McClellan wrote his wife as he packed his bags, "alas for my poor country."

I had been oppressed nearly ever since the battles at Gettysburg, by what appeared to be evidences that yourself, and Gen. Couch, and Gen. Smith, were not seeking a collision with the enemy, but were trying to get him across the river without another battle. ...

—*Excerpt from Lincoln's unsent letter to Meade*

The Search for a Leader Continues

At first it seemed McClellan was correct, as matters seemed to go from bad to worse. Northerners were treated to the disastrous efforts of McClellan's friend and successor, Ambrose Burnside, who orchestrated one of the worst

Union defeats of the war at the Battle of Fredericksburg in December 1862. Burnside was then replaced by Hooker, whose arrogant self-assurance ("may God have mercy on General Lee, for I will have none") led to merely another debacle at the Battle of Chancellorsville in May 1863. Dazed by a cannonball that exploded near his head, Hooker was badly shaken, losing the initiative and eventually the battle itself. When Lincoln read the telegram from the front confirming the Union loss he moaned, "My God! My God! What will the country say?"

A month later, Lee launched his invasion. The president was flooded with advice, condemnation and rumors. Lee was invading Pennsylvania, and because George McClellan was a Pennsylvania native, quite a few people in the Keystone State felt that Lincoln should put McClellan back in charge. "I see no means of resisting the onward march of the Rebels to this city," wrote one breathless correspondent from Philadelphia to Lincoln on June 28, "except through the agency of the Talismatic name of a Pennsylvania General [McClellan] who has the undoubted confidence of her people in his Military capacity."

McClellan was the proverbial elephant in the room as Lee bore down on Gettysburg and the Lincoln administration scrambled to respond. McClellan's emergence as one of the chief national spokesmen for the limited war, anti-emancipationist segment of the Northern populace politicized what was already a difficult situation. On June 30, just as

MAJOR GENL McCLELLAN.

The handsome Gen. McClellan cut a gallant figure and was popular despite his missed opportunities. This made Lincoln's decision to remove him more difficult.

The case, summarily stated is this. You fought and beat the enemy at Gettysburg; and, of course, to say the least, his loss was as great as yours. He retreated; and you did not, as it seemed to me, pressingly pursue him; but a flood in the river detained him, till, by slow degrees, you were again upon him. You had at least twenty thousand veteran troops directly with you, and as many more raw ones within supporting distance, all in addition to those who fought with you at Gettysburg. ...

—*Excerpt from Lincoln's unsent letter to Meade*

the outer elements of Lee's army approached Gettysburg, Congressman William Kelley from Pennsylvania visited Lincoln in the White House and strongly urged the president not to give McClellan a high command, probably reflecting Kelley's status as a stalwart Republican and advocate for black freedom and suffrage. That same morning Lincoln received a telegram from a different Pennsylvania politician, Alexander McClure, who demanded that Lincoln appoint McClellan commander of the army to inspire the populace and rescue the North from "the hopelessness now prevailing."

Lincoln's exasperated response to McClure revealed his impatience with the entire McClellan question. "Do we gain anything by opening one leak to stop another?" he asked. "Do we gain anything by quieting one clamor, merely to open another, and probably a larger one?" The president had crossed a line when he both fired McClellan and embraced an emancipationist vision of the war. There would be no turning back, at least not on his watch. The Young Napoleon remained on the sidelines.

In the meantime, Lincoln had decided to replace Hooker, just four days after that cabinet meeting in which Welles thought the president looked sad. Hooker had never been the same after Chancellorsville, and his incessant requests for reinforcements sounded increasingly McClellan-ish. Hooker's replacement was Gen. George Gordon Meade, a division commander in the Army of the Potomac. Like McClellan, Meade possessed Pennsylvania connections (his father was from Philadelphia), but there the similarities ended. Where McClellan was famously charming, Meade was considerably less so — "a damned old

In this lithograph printed after his assassination, Lincoln is surrounded by (from upper left) Ulysses S. Grant, George Meade, Philip Sheridan and William Tecumseh Sherman.

goggle-eyed snapping turtle," groused one of his subordinates. Meade was solid, unspectacular and steady. He did not mix in politics and he did not excite the extreme passions, both for and against, created by McClellan. He did his job with a lack of dramatic flair that Lincoln probably found refreshing.

Again, my dear general, I do not believe you appreciate the magnitude of the misfortune involved in Lee's escape. He was within your easy grasp, and to have closed upon him would, in connection with our other late successes, have ended the war. As it is, the war will be prolonged indefinitely. If you could not safely attack Lee last Monday, how can you possibly do so south of the river, when you can take with you very few more than two-thirds of the force you then had in hand? It would be unreasonable to expect, and I do not expect you can now effect much. Your golden opportunity is gone, and I am distressed immeasurably because of it.

—Excerpt from Lincoln's unsent letter to Meade

The President in the Telegraph Room

Lincoln installed Meade as commander of the Army of the Potomac on June 28, just as Gen. Lee's army began to cross the Pennsylvania state line. For the next three days, the president conducted business as usual — cabinet meetings, various matters with Congress — as the two massive armies shadowed each other across the Pennsylvania countryside. "We have rumors of hard fighting today," Welles recorded in his diary on July 1.

And then...nothing. Like every other wartime president before and since, Lincoln was condemned to long hours of waiting, watching from afar while others did the actual fighting. There being no direct telegraphic link to the White House, Lincoln habitually crossed the street to the massive brick building that housed the War Department, then made his way up to the second floor and a room that formerly housed the department's library. Here Secretary of War Edwin Stanton installed the army's telegraph machinery adjacent to his own office, along with desks for the cipher-operators who translated news directly from the front.

Lincoln often circulated informally among the operators, reading the dispatches over their shoulders as the news trickled in. If he was compelled to leave for some reason, he would upon returning sift through the stacks of messages that had arrived during his absence until he got to those he had already read. "Well, boys, I am down to raisins," he would remark with a smile, then return to his pacing among the operators.

"He almost lived in the telegraph office when a battle was in progress," remembered an observer; and so it was during the Battle of Gettysburg.

Dispatches from Gettysburg

Welles found him there very early on the morning of July 2. Lincoln apparently spent the entire day there and most of the next. "Hour after hour during those anxious days and nights," recalled an operator, the president scanned the dispatches.

Lincoln with some of the officers leading the eastern Army. McClellan is sixth from the left, facing Lincoln. George Custer, famous for his role in the Battle of the Little Bighorn in 1876, stands at the far right.

Gen. Hooker (left) and Gen. Burnside (below) both failed in brief stints as the head of the Army of the Potomac.

Exactly what he was reading, and how he was reacting, moment to moment, to the scattered reports trickling in from Gettysburg is unknown. Private matters intruded. On July 3, around the time Lee was preparing for Pickett's Charge, Mary Lincoln was injured in a carriage accident. Lincoln felt compelled to telegraph their son Robert at Harvard that his mother was okay. Otherwise, he devoted at least the morning (and quite likely most of the afternoon) to reading telegraph dispatches from the battle. By 10 a.m. the next day he felt confident enough to issue an official proclamation from the White House, declaring "a great success to the cause of the Union."

Meade had won his battle. He would remain the Army of the Potomac's commander for the remainder of the war, though his star would be eclipsed by that of Ulysses S. Grant, whom Lincoln appointed general-in-chief, or overall commander of the Union Army, in March 1864. Lincoln was not in fact entirely pleased with Meade, despite the Gettysburg triumph. What was left of Lee's battered army escaped back into Virginia, with Meade showing no inclination to pursue. Lincoln was livid. "My dear general, I do not believe you appreciate the magnitude of the misfortune involved in Lee's escape. ...Your golden opportunity is gone, and I am distressed immeasureably because of it." Lincoln never sent this message to Meade — who most certainly would have regarded it as a stinging rebuke — but he never entirely trusted the victor of Gettysburg thereafter.

Remembering the Battle

Lincoln did not figure very prominently in the planning for a November 1863 ceremony dedicating Gettysburg National Cemetery. He was asked to attend only as an afterthought. He wasn't even the keynote speaker.

Nevertheless, the president chose his words carefully. Contrary to myth, he did not write the Gettysburg Address on the back of an envelope en route to the battlefield. In fact, he labored for days to get his thoughts exactly correct. In that now-famous 272-word address, lasting just over two minutes, Lincoln gave meaning to the carnage of that awful battle — indeed, of the war itself.

Unlike McClellan, who wanted the war to be as small and insignificant as possible, Lincoln at Gettysburg moved in precisely the opposite direction. Setting aside all the grubby details of the war's daily grind — McClellan's ego, the incompetence of Burnside and Hooker, Meade's shortcomings, those long hours in the telegraph office — Lincoln invoked the deepest themes of American democracy, freedom and self-government.

America had been for eighty-seven years an experiment in "the proposition that all men are created equal," Lincoln declared. "Now we are engaged in a great civil war, testing whether that nation or any nation so conceived and so dedicated, can long endure"—here was an understanding of the war in its deepest sense, with meaning extending beyond the president himself, his generals, the battles, even the North and the South. What was at stake here, Lincoln argued, was nothing less than the answer to the age-old question of whether or not people are capable of governing themselves without descending into chaos. Only in that sense did all of the deaths at Gettysburg have meaning, for Lincoln and for the nation as a whole.

He seemed to know he had spoken profoundly and well in his two-minute speech; the story that both Lincoln and the audience thought the speech a failure ("that speech won't scour," he is supposed to have remarked to a bystander) is largely a myth. The ceremony's keynote speaker, former Harvard president and famed orator Edward Everett, wrote to Lincoln a note of congratulations: "I should be glad if I could flatter myself that I came as near to the central idea of the occasion, in two hours, as you did in two minutes." **G**

Brian Dirck is a professor of history at Anderson University in Indiana. He has written five books on Abraham Lincoln.

At the dedication of the Soldiers' National Cemetery in Gettysburg on November 19, 1863, Lincoln decisively committed the Union toward pursuing a vision of the war as a "new birth of freedom."

The Gettysburg Address

Four score and seven years ago our fathers brought forth on this continent a new nation, conceived in liberty and dedicated to the proposition that all men are created equal.

Now we are engaged in a great civil war, testing whether that nation or any nation so conceived and so dedicated can long endure. We are met on a great battlefield of that war. We have come to dedicate a portion of that field as a final resting place for those who here gave their lives that that nation might live. It is altogether fitting and proper that we should do this.

But in a larger sense, we cannot dedicate, we cannot consecrate, we cannot hallow this ground. The brave men, living and dead, who struggled here have consecrated it far above our poor power to add or detract. The world will little note nor long remember what we say here, but it can never forget what they did here. It is for us the living, rather, to be dedicated here to the unfinished work which they who fought here have thus far so nobly advanced. It is rather for us to be here dedicated to the great task remaining before us — that from these honored dead we take increased devotion to that cause for which they gave the last full measure of devotion — that we here highly resolve that these dead shall not have died in vain, that this nation under God shall have a new birth of freedom, and that government of the people, by the people, for the people shall not perish from the earth.

Father Corby's Absolution

A shared moment of faith, amid the whir of bullets and the crash of cannon, pointed toward a new brotherhood of battle.

By William Burton Kurtz

When the war came, Irish and other ethnic Catholic men joined regiments across the North, bishops raised flags over cathedrals and priests volunteered to serve as chaplains.

Catholics, and particularly Irish Catholics, saw the Civil War as a chance to prove their right to citizenship. Nativist politicians, who saw immigrants and Catholics as a threat to American society, had vigorously assailed their patriotism during the two decades prior to the war.

The most famous of all of the Catholic chaplains of the Civil War is Reverend William Corby, a member of the Congregation of the Holy Cross at Notre Dame in Indiana. When the war began, there was no reason to think that Corby would rise to prominence. He was not the only priest from Notre Dame to serve, nor was he the only chaplain to serve in the famed Irish Brigade of the Army of the Potomac. Certainly many others rivaled Corby in terms of bravery and commitment to the souls of Catholic soldiers.

A statue at the University of Notre Dame honors Father William Corby and is a replica of the statue at Gettysburg.

Corby went from being an obscure Midwestern priest of Irish ancestry to a war hero because of the Battle of Gettysburg. As the cannon thunder at Pickett's Charge faded into memory, Gettysburg grew in importance in the eyes of most Americans, both Northerners and Southerners, who came to view it as the turning point of the war. Northern Catholic veterans, like others who served, were intent on reminding the nation about their wartime service. Catholic veterans, including Corby, knew that their best chance of highlighting their faith community's contributions to victory lay in staking their own unique claim to Gettysburg.

An Irish Chaplain

Corby was born in Detroit on October 2, 1833. His father was an Irish immigrant who was a wealthy businessman and patron of local Irish-Catholic churches. Corby attended Notre Dame, and by 1860 had become a priest in the Congregation of the Holy Cross. In the fall of 1861, Corby became the chaplain of the 88th New York Infantry Regiment. This unit was part of the famous Irish Brigade of the Union Army of the Potomac.

As Corby wrote in his *Memoirs of Chaplain Life*, his duties in camp were not much different from when he was at home serving in a parish: "*We*

The Irish Brigade monument at Gettysburg.

"Let us hope that many thousands of souls, purified by hardships, fasting, prayer, and blood, met a favorable sentence on the ever memorable battlefield of Gettysburg."

celebrated Mass, heard confessions, preached on Sundays and holydays. During the week, many minor duties occupied us. We were called on at times to administer the pledge to a few who had been indulging too freely, to settle little difficulties, and encourage harmony and good-will; to instruct such as needed private lessons on special points of religion, and everywhere to elevate the standard of religion, morality, and true patriotism."

Catholic chaplains were often in short supply, so Corby would visit other regiments and hospitals to take care of the spiritual welfare of Catholics in the army. Although a chaplain, he shared many of the hardships of the enlisted men: muddy marches, freezing winter camps, perpetual illness. Corby insisted that he and his fellow chaplains stay as close to the fighting as they could in order to administer to dying men. He was proud of the fact that of the hundreds of men who died during the Seven Days Battles, "almost...none [died] without having shortly before received the sacraments."

By the summer of 1863, Corby was the only priest still actively serving in the Irish Brigade. The war's daily grind and camp illnesses had sent the others home, some temporarily, some for good. This made his task almost impossible, even though the Irish Brigade was reduced to an effective strength of less than a regiment due to the terrible casualties it had sustained at the battles of Antietam, Fredericksburg and Chancellorsville.

The Absolution

The Battle of Gettysburg in July would prove to be another bloody engagement for Corby's men, who saw action on the second day of the battle in the middle of the Union line, in the area that became known as the Wheatfield. Just before the brigade went into action, Corby asked for a halt so he could say a general absolution because "our men...had had absolutely no chance to practise their religious duties during the past two or three weeks, being constantly on the march."

Absolution, for Catholics, is part of the sacrament of penance. The penitent confesses his sins and the priest, upon hearing the confession,

Father Corby (seated on right) sits next to his fellow chaplain and Notre Dame priest, James Dillon, and other members of the Irish Brigade.

absolves the penitent of those sins. A general absolution is reserved for occasions when, due to imminent danger of death, it is impossible for a priest to hear each confession individually. If ever death was imminent it was to those men: They were about to take part in the futile effort to control the Peach Orchard, the scene of some of the heaviest fighting on the second day of battle at Gettysburg.

In Corby's memoirs, his friend, Gen. St. Clair A. Mulholland, wrote: "Now (as the Third Corps is being pressed back), help is called for. 'Fall in!' and the men run to their places. …The Irish Brigade…whose green flag has been unfurled in every battle in which the Army of the Potomac had been engaged…stood in column of regiments, closed in mass. As a large majority of its members were Catholics, the Chaplain of the brigade, Rev. William Corby, proposed to give a general absolution to all the men before going into the fight. While this is customary in the armies of Catholic countries in Europe, it was perhaps the first time it was ever witnessed on this continent. …Father Corby stood on a large rock in front of the brigade. Addressing the

FIGHTING NEXT TO A NEIGHBOR

Before the Civil War, the standing professional army consisted of only 16,000 regulars. Most Northern soldiers enlisted as volunteers into brand-new regiments that were organized by state. Volunteers could choose which of their state's new regiments they joined; different regiments had different officers, chaplains and monetary inducements paid to encourage men to enlist. Often volunteers chose to serve in regiments raised from their city or county so that they could fight alongside their friends and neighbors. In heavily populated areas, they could even choose to enlist in regiments with a particular ethnic identity, such as regiments composed mainly of Irish or German immigrants.

Officers of the 69th New York, one of the regiments in the Irish Brigade.

Officers of 69th New York State Militia, Fort Corcoran, Va.

men, he explained what he was about to do, saying that each one could receive the benefit of the absolution by making a sincere Act of Contrition. ...As he closed his address, every man, Catholic and non-Catholic, fell on his knees with his head bowed down. Then, stretching his right hand toward the brigade, Father Corby pronounced the words of the absolution."

Mulholland described the scene as "awe-inspiring." He went on to write: "Nearby stood a brilliant throng of officers who had gathered to witness this very unusual occurrence, and while there was profound silence in the ranks of the Second Corps, yet over to the left, out by the peach orchard and Little Round Top, where Weed and Vincent and Hazlitt were dying, the roar of the battle rose and swelled and re-echoed through the woods,

making music more sublime than ever sounded through the cathedral aisle. The act seemed to be in harmony with the surroundings. I do not think there was a man in the brigade who did not offer up a heart-felt prayer. For some, it was their last; they knelt there in their grave clothes. In less than half an hour many of them were numbered with the dead of July 2. Who can doubt that their prayers were good? What was wanting in the eloquence of the priest to move them to repentance was supplied in the incidents of the fight. That heart would be incorrigible, indeed, that the scream of a Whitworth bolt, added to Father Corby's touching appeal, would not move to contrition."

Corby's absolution has since become one of the most famous religious moments of the entire Civil War. When Protestant soldiers joined

Corby insisted that he and his fellow chaplains stay as close to the fighting as they could in order to administer to dying men.

Catholics in kneeling to receive the blessing, their spontaneous action seemed to show how the shared experience of combat and its horrors broke down religious barriers between Union soldiers. Their common prayer across denominational lines served as a rebuke to anti-immigrant and anti-Catholic sentiment. Such an unusual event promised a greater level of religious tolerance following the conflict, born from the shared shedding of blood of Americans of all creeds alike.

Corby Remembers the Absolution

While July 2 was the first instance that Corby gave absolution on a battlefield, it was (unknown to Gen. Mulholland) not the first time that it had happened during the Civil War. Unable to hear the confessions of everyone wanting to see him before the First Battle of Bull Run in July 1861, Father Paul Gillen, another Notre Dame priest, had given general absolution to soldiers still waiting in line shortly before the fighting had begun. Father Peter Paul Cooney, also of Corby's order, likewise gave absolution to the men of the 35th Indiana as they marched toward the battlefield of Stones River, Tennessee in late 1862.

Corby himself later admitted to a friend that he had kept no diary or record of the event from the war. Still, the act of giving absolution at Gettysburg became a defining part of his later life. Corby wrote in his memoirs: *"In performing this ceremony I faced the army. My eye covered thousands of officers and men. I noticed that all, Catholic and non-Catholic, officers and private soldiers showed a profound respect, wishing at this fatal crisis to receive every benefit of divine grace that could be imparted through the instrumentality of the Church ministry. Even Maj.-Gen. Hancock removed his hat, and, as far as compatible with the situation, bowed in reverential devotion. That general absolution was intended for all—in quantum possum—not only for our brigade, but for all, North or*

THE IRISH BRIGADE

Michael Corcoran, leader of the 69th New York.

LIBRARY OF CONGRESS

The Irish Brigade is one of the most famous units in the Union Army. Its core regiments were the 69th New York, the 63rd New York, the 88th New York, the 28th Massachusetts and the 116th Pennsylvania.

Initial recruitment targeted Irish Catholics by appealing to their sense of loyalty to both Ireland and the Union. Local Irish-American political leaders such as Thomas Meagher became officers, while many of the rank and file were recent immigrants to the United States who had fled the Irish Potato Famine of the 1840s.

Serving with fellow Catholic Irishmen was appealing for a number of reasons. First, some volunteers wanted military experience for a future war of Irish liberation against England. Second, by serving in an Irish unit, the men could avoid anti-Irish sentiment sometimes found in other regiments — while also proving once and for all that Irish immigrants were just as patriotic as soldiers of Protestant or Anglo-Saxon heritage. Third, they would have Catholic priests as chaplains during the war.

While most members of the Irish Brigade were both Catholic and Irish, not every member of the brigade fit into those two groups. The 116th Pennsylvania was perhaps the least Irish of the core units, with other immigrants and native-born Americans serving in it. There were a number of Irish Protestants who joined the brigade in order to serve with their countrymen despite their religious differences. Hard-pressed to replenish its losses, the regiment's replacements were not always Irish. Temporary units assigned to the brigade such as the 29th Massachusetts (which left after Antietam) and the 7th New York Heavy Artillery (which joined late in the war) were not Irish at all.

Still, the brigade's Irish-born officers, its distinctive green flags, its famous St. Patrick's Days celebrations, its Catholic chaplains and the initial core of Irish men who made up the unit ensured that its name was well-deserved. The brigade was known to go into battle shouting "faugh-a-bellagh" (clear the way) and some of their green regimental flags displayed the motto "riam nar druid o sbarin lann" (who never retreated from the clash of spears).

Irish-American newspapers across the country covered the brigade's exploits closely and praised its men and officers for their bravery and patriotism. The unit's reputation for bravery was earned at many of the Army of the Potomac's greatest battles, including Antietam, Fredericksburg and Chancellorsville. The brigade suffered more casualties than almost every other Union brigade and lost two men in combat for every one man who died of disease, the opposite of the ratio for the Union Army as a whole.

The Irish Brigade was famous for its Saint Patrick's Day festivities, which included horse races.

South, who were susceptible of it and who were about to appear before their Judge. Let us hope that many thousands of souls, purified by hardships, fasting, prayer, and blood, met a favorable sentence on the ever memorable battlefield of Gettysburg. …The Irish Brigade had very many advantages over other organizations, as it was at no time during the war without a chaplain; but I was the only one at the battle of Gettysburg. Often in camp and sometimes on the march we held very impressive religious services, but the one at Gettysburg was more public and was witnessed by many who had not, perhaps, seen the others. The surroundings there, too made a vast difference, for really the situation reminded one of the day of judgment, when shall be seen 'men withering away for fear and expectation of what shall come upon the whole world,' so great were the whirlwinds of war then in motion."

In Corby's memory and memoirs, his absolution was unique from others performed during the war for two major reasons. First, it took place in the middle of the most important battle of the Civil War. This ensured that the memory of the battlefield absolution would live on as an important event in Americans' memory of this decisive battle and the war itself. Second, the absolution was generously proclaimed for the men of both armies regardless of their faith. The respect that everyone showed to-

ward Corby, including the Protestant commander of the 2nd Corps, Gen. Hancock, was a lesson in how true patriotism trumped Americans' religious differences. When Corby published his *Memoirs of Chaplain Life* in 1893, his retelling of the absolution spoke to a desire held by many in the North and South for reconciliation between the two sections.

After the War

In 1864, Corby's superiors ordered him to return to Notre Dame, where he twice served as president of the university. Corby held many positions of authority at Notre Dame and the Holy Cross

A FAR CRY FROM ST. PATRICK'S DAY

Irish immigrants were subjected to a level of prejudice unimaginable today. The phrase "No Irish Need Apply" could be found in prewar job advertisements. The Irish were subjected to derogatory slurs such as "papist" and "paddy." Cartoons compared Irishmen to apes.

Order in his eminently successful postwar career. After helping to say a mass at the unveiling of the Irish Brigade Memorial at the 25th anniversary of the Battle of Gettysburg in 1888, Corby joined other Union veterans in commemorating their wartime experiences. Encouraged by his friends from the Irish Brigade, Corby joined many veterans' organizations, including the Grand Army of the Republic (GAR), a prominent organization of Civil War veterans.

Some of Father Corby's old brigade friends started a petition to give him a Medal of Honor. The War Department ultimately declined, stating that the absolution did not fall strictly under the "law authorizing issue of medals." Corby founded GAR Post No. 569 in 1897. It was made up entirely of Catholic priests and brothers. Newspapers across the country, including *The New York Times*, *The Washington Post* and *The Atlanta Constitution* covered the story and published an engraving of Corby and the other men of the post.

In 1897, still as active as ever in his Civil War activities, Corby passed away. Friends and supporters of his memory erected a statue of him in 1910 on the Gettysburg battlefield. It depicts Corby standing on a rock with his right arm extended in the act of giving absolution to his men. Ⓖ

The kneeling troops who received the absolution were preparing to enter the pitched battle to preserve the Union position at the Peach Orchard.

The
Wou

A Union surgeon surveys a field hospital for Confederate wounded after the Battle of Antietam in 1862.

Advances in weapon technology resulted in devastating injuries during the Civil War, creating unimaginable conditions and horrors for surgeons and soldiers.

By Martin Roy Hill

nds of War

By the morning of July 4, 1863, the fighting at Gettysburg had stopped. The suffering and dying had not.

Strewn across the fields of Pickett's Charge, hidden in the long grass of the Wheatfield and trapped amid the boulders of the Devil's Den were the broken, ruptured bodies of the wounded. The relative silence that followed the boom of battle was punctuated by the cries of men tortured by thirst and the pain of their wounds.

"This is a horrid night," Confederate Lt. John Dooley wrote on the night of July 3, "cold and wet and rainy. Groans and shrieks and maniacal ravings; bitter sobs, and heavy sighs, piteous cries; horrid oaths, despair; the death rattle; darkness, death."

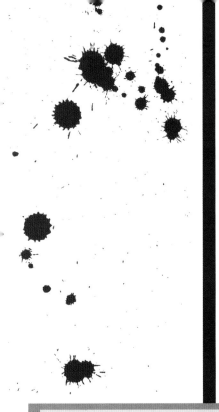

"No written nor expressed language could ever picture the field of Gettysburg!" Union surgeon Bushrod James wrote during the weeks following the battle. "Blood! Blood! And tattered flesh! Shattered bones and mangled forms almost without the semblance of human beings! Faces torn and bruised and lacerated."

Gettysburg was the bloodiest battle of the Civil War. More than 23,000 Union soldiers and as many as 28,000 Confederates became casualties, with over 7,000 killed between the two sides. On that fourth morning in July, many of the wounded still lay where they fell.

New Lethal Weapons

The carnage at Gettysburg was so massive in part because of new technologies designed to maim and kill. As Maj. Gen. George Pickett's men marched up the long incline to Cemetery Ridge, they were met with a hailstorm of modern artillery fire — exploding shells filled with shrapnel and canister shot — followed by highly accurate rifle fire using the new Minié ball.

Prior to the Civil War, soldiers had to be in very close range of each other to use their smooth bore muskets. Napoleonic battlefield tactics involved moving large masses of men, standing shoulder to shoulder, around the battlefield until they faced each other no more than 30 yards apart. The forces would fire one or two volleys at each other, followed by a bayonet

Union Army ambulances clear wounded from the battlefield. It's believed this photo was taken near Fredericksburg, Virginia, in 1862. A two-person, two-wheeled Finley ambulance is seen in the foreground at the far right.

charge. As a result, most combat injuries consisted of stabbing and slashing wounds from bayonets and sabers.

The Minié ball changed all that. Originally designed in 1849 by French Army Captain Claude-Etienne Minié, the Minié ball was conical with a concave bottom. With a diameter smaller than that of the barrel, the Minié ball made loading easier and faster, increasing a soldier's firing rate. When the weapon was fired, gases in the barrel expanded the base of the bullet, digging the projectile's sides into the barrel rifling. This increased both accuracy and distance, putting an end to Napoleonic tactics.

As a result, injuries from bladed weapons accounted for only 5 percent of combat wounds during the Civil War, while Minié bullets were responsible for 85 percent of all wounds. The remaining 10 percent of injuries were caused by artillery.

Wounds created by Minié balls were devastating. Though slow moving compared to today's high-velocity, metal-jacketed bullets, the soft, large-caliber lead Minié rounds would flatten on impact, smashing through tissue and splintering bone. Wounds to the torso were more often than not fatal. Wounds to the arms and legs would shatter an average of six to 10 inches of bone, leaving the limb too badly mangled to repair. Amputation was the usual result.

LIBRARY OF CONGRESS

In this posed photograph, surgeons with a Union zouave regiment prepare to amputate a soldier's arm.

MEDICAL ARTIFACTS

Typically, each ambulance carried two water kegs like this.

MED. DEPT.

PHOTO COURTESY OF THE NATIONAL MUSEUM OF CIVIL WAR MEDICINE

Battlefield artillery had also changed, moving from short-range, smooth-bore cannon that fired solid ball shot to long-range rifled guns firing explosive rounds filled with shrapnel capable of dismembering a soldier in an instant. When the enemy came closer, artillerymen would switch to canister shot, large ball-bearing-like projectiles similar to buckshot from a shotgun. At Gettysburg, Union artillerists learned to aim low and in front of the attacking Confederates, causing the canister shot to ricochet into their legs, often ripping limb from body.

First Aid Stations and Field Hospitals

If the wounded at Gettysburg had anything to be thankful for, it was that battlefield casualty care had made great strides during the war, particularly in the Union Army. At the beginning of the war, there was little organized care for the wounded. First aid stations and hospitals were set up in buildings of opportunity such as churches, barns or homes, often miles from the front lines. There was no organized way of collecting casualties. Lightly wounded soldiers had to walk to the aid station; the more seriously injured had to be carried by their comrades.

During the Battle of Fort Donelson in 1862, Maj. Gen. Ulysses S. Grant's division surgeon, Henry Hewitt, ordered his regimental surgeons to move their aid stations close enough to the fighting to share the "fortunes and dangers" of the common soldier. This change became the model for today's battalion aid station, a highly maneuverable treatment station that sets up sometimes only yards from the fighting.

Another of Grant's surgeons, Bernard John Dowling Irwin, realized too many wounded soldiers were dying while being transported north after surgery. Field hospitals set up in buildings of opportunity rarely had room for recovering soldiers. Men lay in the open, exposed to the elements until they were placed on wagons that took them to Navy riverboats for the trip north. More often than not, the wounded soldiers received no medical care during the entire trip. Weakened by their wounds and exposure to the elements, many soldiers succumbed before reaching Union territory.

The dismembered corpse of a Confederate soldier at Gettysburg shows the effects of Civil War artillery on the combatants.

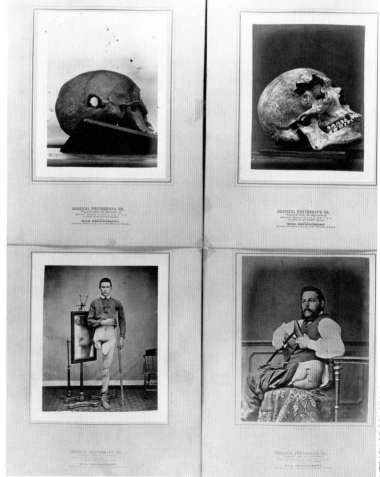

These graphic photographs show the devastating damage done by the weapons of the Civil War.

During the Battle of Shiloh, Irwin created the first true field hospital by acquiring several large captured rebel tents and organizing them into treatment areas, with one tent for first aid, another for surgery and several for post-surgical ward care. In the ward tents, wounded soldiers were given food, drink and time to recover before being evacuated. Irwin saw his patients' survival rates soar.

Triage and the Ambulance Corps

Union Major Jonathan Letterman, medical director for the Army of the Potomac, took the lessons learned by Hewitt and Irwin, as well as the knowledge learned during the Napoleonic and Crimean Wars, and developed the first integrated battlefield medical evacuation system. Besides adopting Irwin's field hospital, Letterman instituted the practice of triage, or sorting patients by prioritizing their care based on their injuries. He also established the Army Ambulance Corps, with wagons specially designed to transport the

CARE FOR THEIR ENEMIES

Both sides treated the wounded of their opponents. Confederate Capt. Decimus et Ultimus Barziza of the 4th Texas Regiment was wounded on July 2 and taken to the field hospital of the Union's 12th Army Corps. "Our wounded were generally well treated, and we were put side by side with the enemy's," he wrote. "The surgeons, with sleeves rolled up and blood to the elbows, were continually employed in amputating limbs. The red, human blood ran in streams from under the operating tables, and huge piles of arms and legs, withered and horrible to behold, were mute evidences of the fierceness of the strife."

Surgeons used the same implements to operate on multiple patients with no more cleaning than a wipe across their bloody smocks.

MEDICAL ARTIFACTS

Ether, used as an anesthetic during surgery.

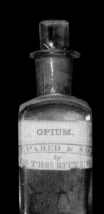

Opium, used for pain relief.

A battlefield amputation kit; a tourniquet is on the lower left.

PHOTOS COURTESY OF THE NATIONAL MUSEUM OF CIVIL WAR MEDICINE

wounded. Long-range transport was accomplished with the first hospital ships and trains.

Gettysburg was the first major battle to test Letterman's new system. As the Union Army approached Gettysburg, it had about 650 medical officers and more than 1,000 ambulances. Each division had a medical director, who established a field hospital at the rear of his division. Each field hospital had three surgeons and three nonsurgical medical officers. Each regiment had a medical officer plus an assistant, who established their aid station as close to the fighting as possible. Ambulances consisted of two-wheeled Finleys and four-wheeled Triplers, equipped to carry two or four patients, respectively.

The Confederate Army medical system was similarly arranged. At Gettysburg, however, Gen. Robert E. Lee's army had only about 400 doctors and no ambulances. Common wagons were used to transport the wounded.

While the organization of casualty care had greatly advanced during the war, the actual

"Blood! Blood! And tattered flesh! Shattered bones and mangled forms almost without the semblance of human beings!"

practice of medicine had not. Contrary to popular myth, anesthetic agents such as ether and chloroform were widely used by both armies during the Civil War. Morphine, opium and whiskey were the chief painkillers. However, due to Operation Anaconda — the Union Navy's blockade of Southern ports — medications, including anesthetics, were chronically in short supply in the Confederacy. Wounded gray coats frequently had little to counter the pain of surgery.

The wounded are collected by lamplight following the Battle of Hatcher's Run in 1865. After the last day of battle at Gettysburg, litter bearers scoured the battlefield for the wounded of both sides, often led through the dark by the cries of the injured.

LIBRARY OF CONGRESS

Slaughterhouses

The surgeons on both sides performed their best under trying circumstances, but the medical knowledge they had was severely lacking by modern standards. There were no aseptic operating rooms. Instruments were not sterilized. Surgeons used the same implements to operate on multiple patients with no more cleaning than a wipe across their bloody smocks. They sliced away flesh from wounded limbs using the same scalpel over and over again. To save time, they kept the bone saw used for amputations at the ready by clenching it in their teeth. Sepsis and gangrene led to slow, agonizing deaths for many of the wounded.

On the first day of the battle, as Brig. Gen. John Buford's Union troops fought their stalling action against the Confederates, hospitals were hastily thrown up in several Gettysburg churches. Reuben Ruch, a wounded Union soldier, was taken to the Trinity German Reformed Church. "I found the (church) full," he later wrote. "I should call it a slaughter house. There must have been 10 to 12 amputation tables in (one) room ... they were all busy. The doctors had their sleeves rolled up to their shoulders and were covered in blood."

As the two armies converged on Gettysburg, the medical systems of each adversary went into full action. Litter bearers braved shot and shell to remove casualties; many became casualties themselves. Ambulance crews sortied back and

CIVIL WAR MEDICINE ON DISPLAY

If the Civil War, historic implements and medical history intrigue you, then head to historic downtown Frederick, Maryland, and visit the National Museum of Civil War Medicine. The museum is centrally located within a 35-minute drive to several key Civil War battlefields, including Antietam, South Mountain and Monocacy in Maryland; Gettysburg in Pennsylvania; and Harpers Ferry in West Virginia.

Allot between 45 minutes and two hours to tour the museum.

The National Museum of Civil War Medicine, located at 48 East Patrick Street, is open from 10 a.m. to 5 p.m. Thursday through Saturday, and 11 a.m. to 5 p.m. on Sunday.

For more information, call 301-695-1864, or check www.civilwarmed.org.

MEDICAL ARTIFACTS

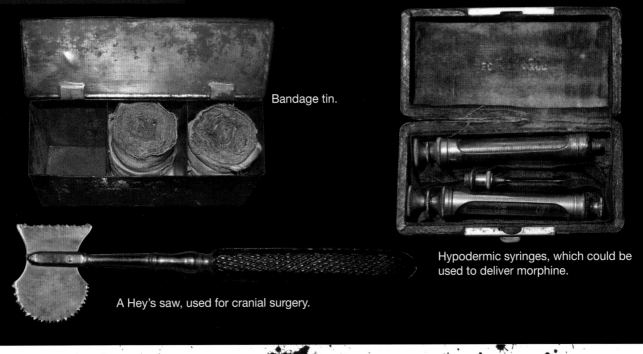

Bandage tin.

Hypodermic syringes, which could be used to deliver morphine.

A Hey's saw, used for cranial surgery.

PHOTOS COURTESY OF THE NATIONAL MUSEUM OF CIVIL WAR MEDICINE

Dr. Jonathan Letterman, medical director for the Army of the Potomac, poses with his staff. Letterman (second from left, seated) was a major innovator in the organization of casualty care.

forth, carrying wounded to aid stations and the field hospitals, then returning to the front to take on more of their gruesome cargo.

Suffering After the Battle

By nightfall on July 4, most of the wounded had been cleared from the battlefield and transported to field hospitals. Unfortunately, on July 6 the Union Army quickly uprooted to follow the retreating Confederates. With the army went most of the surgeons. Only 106 Union surgeons and a handful of Confederate surgeons were left to care for tens of thousands of wounded men. "No more could be left," Letterman wrote in his official report, "as it was expected that another battle would, within three or four days, take place; and, in all probability, as many wounded be thrown upon our hands as at the battle of the 2d and 3d."

The suffering continued for weeks. The small number of Union and Confederate surgeons, aug-

mented with contracted and volunteer surgeons, worked relentlessly, amputating limbs reeking of gangrene and cleaning and redressing suppurating wounds.

"Groans and cries, screams, and curses, moans and grinding teeth!" surgeon James recalled. "And the horrible silence of torture beyond all expression those weeks of sickening work, when the cut of the knife and the rasp of the saw grated on my overtaxed nerves."

On July 22, Camp Letterman, a large, central field hospital, opened a mile northeast of Gettysburg, close to the railroad. The camp had 400 tents holding 12 beds each. Yankee and rebel wounded shared tents.

There were only 40 surgeons to treat the wounded at Camp Letterman. Nevertheless, some 4,000 casualties passed through the hospital between July and November, when it closed. Twice daily, hospital trains moved the wounded from

Camp Letterman to hospitals throughout the North. About 1,200 men remain buried at the site.

The final casualties of the Battle of Gettysburg were taken northward on November 19, the same day President Lincoln arrived to give his iconic speech. Many of those who survived their wounds would suffer for the rest of their lives. Missing limbs and disfigured faces were only part of the postwar legacy. Without modern antibiotics and aseptic techniques, many wounds never fully healed. They would repeatedly reopen or become infected again, plaguing the survivors for the rest of their lives.

Nevertheless, despite poor training and a lack of modern understanding of wounds, the surgeons and their attendants at the Battle of Gettysburg did a masterful job of saving lives. According to Letterman's account, 14,193 wounded men were treated in Union field hospitals. More than 12,000 more casualties were treated in Confederate field hospitals that were not as well supplied as the Union's.

The suffering continued for weeks. The small number of… surgeons…worked relentlessly, amputating limbs reeking of gangrene and cleaning and redressing suppurating wounds.

"The conduct of the medical officers was admirable," Letterman concluded in his official report. "Their labors not only began with the beginning of the battle, but lasted long after the battle had ended. When other officers had time to rest, they were busily at work — and not merely at work, but working earnestly and devotedly." Ⓖ

MEDICAL ARTIFACTS

Mercurial ointment, used for skin treatment, syphilis and to kill body lice.

A pocket surgical kit, which contained small versions of the tools a surgeon used most often.

A small folding drug kit with morphine, quinine, lead acetate, ipecac and opium, among others.

PHOTOS COURTESY OF THE NATIONAL MUSEUM OF CIVIL WAR MEDICINE

The Bad Old Man of Gettysburg

By Kenneth Weisbrode

Jubal Early,

a Virginian and Confederate, was known for his mixed battle record in the Shenandoah and for an awful disposition. He has been described by the historian Samuel Eliot Morison as "a snarling misanthrope, bent by arthritis contracted in the Mexican War, but eager and aggressive." Robert E. Lee called Early "my bad old man." Early himself confessed that he was

> *never blessed with popular or captivating manners, and the consequence was that I was often misjudged and thought to be haughty and disdainful in my temperament. When earnestly engaged about my business, in passing through a crowd I would frequently pass an acquaintance without noticing him, because of the preoccupation of my mind, and this often gave offence. From all of which it resulted that I was never what is called a popular man. I can say, however, that those who knew me best, liked me best, and the prejudices against me were gradually wearing off as the people became better acquainted with me.*

"Old Jube," as he was known to his troops, graduated from West Point in 1837. He finished near the middle of his class and was noted mainly for a dispute with a fellow cadet who broke a plate over Early's head. Early received a commission, but left the army shortly thereafter to practice law. He returned briefly to the army as a volunteer in the Mexican War, but did little to distinguish himself.

Law and Politics

Evidently he did not think much of a military career for himself: "I was not a very exemplary soldier...I had very little taste for scrubbing brass, and cared very little for the advancement to be obtained by the exercise of that most useful art." His interests were in winning cases as a prosecutor and in entering politics as a member of the Virginia legislature. He was a strong defender of the Southern way of life, including the institution of slavery. Northerners were free to debate it in theory, but Early felt they had maligned it in practice by distortion and insult.

> During the war, slavery was used as a catch-word to arouse the passions of a fanatical mob, and to some extent the prejudices of the civilized world were excited against us; but the war was not made on our part for slavery.
>
> High dignitaries in both church and state in Old England, and puritans in New England, had participated in the profits of a trade by which the ignorant and barbarous natives of Africa were brought from that country and sold into slavery in the American Colonies. The generation in the Southern States which defended their country in the late war, found amongst them, in a civilized and Christianized condition, 4,000,000 of the descendants of those...Africans. The Creator of the Universe had stamped them, indelibly, with a different color. ...He had not done this from mere caprice or whim, but for wise purposes. An amalgamation of the races was in contravention of His designs or He would not have made them so different.

"Nevertheless," Early insisted, "the struggle made by the people of the South was not for the institution of slavery, but for the inestimable right of self-government, against the domination of a fanatical faction at the North; and slavery was the mere occasion of the development of the antagonism between the two sections. That right of self-government has been lost, and slavery violently abolished."

Secession

Like Lee, Early had not been an ardent promoter of secession but remained loyal to his state once secession came.

> When the question of practical secession from the United States arose, as a citizen of the State of Virginia, and a member of the Convention called by the authority of the Legislature of that State, I opposed secession with all the ability I possessed, with the hope that the horrors of civil war might be averted and that a returning sense of justice on the part of the masses of the Northern States would induce them to respect the rights of the people of the South. ...While some Northern politicians and editors were openly and sedulously justifying and encouraging secession, I was laboring honestly and earnestly to preserve the Union.

Having failed, Early cast his lot with his beloved state. Early's command record included the battles of Bull Run, Williamsburg, Cedar Mountain, Antietam, Fredericksburg and Chancellorsville. Despite a notable loss at Williamsburg, where he was wounded, he earned a reputation as a tough and aggressive commander.

Cemetery Hill

At Gettysburg, Early served under Lt. Gen. Richard Ewell. Earlier in the Gettysburg campaign, Early had captured the town and demanded a ransom for it after having entered, it was said, sporting "a glossy black ostrich feather, in beautiful condition" on his hat. During the battle his division was mainly occupied in the siege of Cemetery Hill, concentrating on the right end of the Union line.

His initial plan to attack Cemetery Hill during the night of the first day of fighting and into the early morning was thwarted when Ewell decided against it. When it took place on the following day, it did not succeed.

Early wrote that a decisive Confederate victory at Gettysburg may have been obtained "by a prompt advance of all the troops that had been engaged on our side against the hill upon and behind which the enemy had taken refuge, but a common superior did not happen to be present, and the opportunity was lost." He went on to write, "The only troops engaged on our side were Hill's two divisions and Ewell's two divisions, the rest of the army not being up."

For that Early named a principal culprit:

> The general attack was not made...because there was great delay in the arrival of Longstreet's corps, and on the left Rodes' and my divisions remained in position until late in the afternoon, waiting for the preparations on the right.
>
> This battle of Gettysburg has been much criticised, and will continue to be criticised. Errors were undoubtedly committed, but these errors were not attributable to General Lee. I know that he was exceedingly anxious to attack the enemy at a very early hour on the morning of the 2nd, for I heard him earnestly express that wish on the evening previous, but his troops did not arrive in time to make the attack.

"My loss in the three days' fighting at Gettysburg was 158 killed, 796 wounded, and 227 missing, a large proportion of the missing being, in all probability, killed or wounded. The enemy's loss at the points where [my] brigades were engaged far exceeded my loss, and a very large number of prisoners were secured."

— from Early's official report on the Battle of Gettysburg

Scared Lincoln Like Hell

Early is best known for his raid in July 1864 that came within a few miles of Washington, D.C. and brought panic to the population of the capital, including, reportedly, to Lincoln himself, who observed Early's troops from the top of Fort Stevens and stood within shooting range. This was the final significant incursion of Confederate forces into the territory of the North and did much to damage morale there, even at this late stage of the war. "We haven't taken Washington," he was reported to have said, "but we scared Abe Lincoln like hell!"

Early may well have succeeded in conquering the capital had it not been for the delay he had suffered at Monocacy Junction on account of troops under the command of Gen. Lew Wallace. Early also blamed the heat, drought and "a suffocating cloud of dust," as well as fortifications and skirmishing, which removed the element of surprise.

Early's army was a fraction of the Union force arrayed against it that ultimately held off his raid. His success managed to keep large amounts of Union troops on the defensive, thereby prolonging the end of the war, according to some estimates, by as long as nine months. "A glance at the map," Early concluded, "when it is recollected that the Potomac is a wide river, and navigable to Washington with the largest vessels, will cause the intelligent reader to wonder, not why I failed to take Washington, but why I had the audacity to approach it as I did, with the small force under my command."

Later in life, Early became a leading romanticizer of the antebellum South.

After the War

Following the war, Early refused to swear loyalty to the Union and lived for a time as an exile in Mexico and Canada until he was pardoned by President Andrew Johnson. He spent the remainder of his years back in Lynchburg nursing various feuds against the North and fellow commanders, notably Longstreet, whom he blamed more than anyone else for the South's defeat. He also became one of the principal boosters of the Lost Cause, a romantic, idealized view of the South as a separate nation with a separate way of life. According to this view, the South was defeated but not dishonored, and may have survived had the balance of resources not been tilted so much in the North's favor.

Early felt the cause and campaign themselves were just, and Gen. Lee blameless: "I knew that in everything he did as commander of our armies, General Lee was actuated solely by an earnest and ardent desire for the success of the cause of his country. As to those among my countrymen who judged me harshly, I have not a word of reproach."

In fact Early became one of Lee's principal hagiographers, enveloping his character and legacy with the romance, virtue and tragedy of the Old South. He was the founder of the Southern Historical Society and did much to shape the memory and legacy of the war in the South. Among other qualities, Early was known for his prodigious memory and powers of persuasion, and for the detail contained in his book, *A Memoir of the Last Year of the War for Independence,* published in 1867. This was the first book of its kind published by a significant military commander of the war, and remains one of the most vivid of that genre. It was followed later by his *Autobiographical Sketch and Narrative of the War Between the States,* from which the above excerpts were taken. **ⓖ**

A Life Spared

The exact number of casualties at Gettysburg is unknown. Historians estimate that each side suffered between 20,000 and 25,000 casualties — men killed, wounded or missing. The total number of dead from the Civil War as a whole is likewise the subject of debate: Somewhere between 600,000 and 750,000 soldiers died during the course of the war, out of about 3 million total soldiers — North and South — who fought.

The numbers are at once awe-inspiring and abstract. The difference between a long life as a veteran and death as a soldier was, of course, mostly up to fate.

The following excerpt from *African American Faces of the Civil War* presents a thumbnail sketch of one man's life. He was on his way south and would likely have fought at Gettysburg but was sent to New York instead. Later he watched Lincoln's triumphant entrance into Richmond. Personal tragedy hit later in his life. He died in 1921 at the age of 83, 60 years after he first went to war.

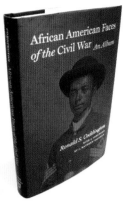

"I was born under the regime of slavery, a free child, my mother being a free woman," explained North Carolina–born Alexander Newton, "My father was a slave, so that in my family, I learned what slavery was. I felt its curse in my bones and I longed for an opportunity and the power to play the part of a Moses in behalf of my people. I suppose this was the wild dream of every child born during slavery."

Flash forward to April 12, 1861. The bombardment of Fort Sumter signaled the start of war — and for Newton an opportunity to realize his boyhood dream. "My bosom burst with the fire of patriotism for the salvation of my country and my people," he declared. At the time he lived in Brooklyn, New York, headquarters of the Thirteenth New York National Guard Infantry. It mobilized for duty within days after the attack. Newton could not enlist because of the color of his skin. "The United States was not taking Negro troops," he noted, without further comment, in his autobiography.

The policy did not stop him. On April 23, 1861, when the Thirteenth left for Washington, D.C., to protect the capital, Newton went with them. He may have served as an officer's valet or in another supporting role.

The regiment made it as far as Annapolis, Maryland, when federal authorities ordered it to Baltimore to maintain law and order among the city's pro-South populace. The New Yorkers left Baltimore in August 1861, after the expiration of their three-month term of enlistment. The Thirteenth was activated again for brief stints in 1862 and 1863. Evidence suggests that Newton accompanied the regiment both times.

The latter mobilization, organized to resist the Confederate invasion of the North that ended with the Battle of Gettysburg, ended prematurely after New York State officials recalled the regiment to quell draft riots in New York City. The Thirteenth arrived a day after the angry mobs were broken up. Violent protestors intent on harassing blacks still roamed the streets, however. Fearing for his life, Newton fled the city.

He wound up in New Haven, Connecticut. By this time the Emancipation Proclamation and a series of congressional acts enabled black men to join the army. Newton enlisted in the Twenty-ninth Connecticut Infantry in December 1863. He received an appointment as second sergeant in Company E.

This carte de visite image of Alexander Newton, left, and Daniel Lathrop is engraved on a monument honoring the 29th Connecticut Volunteer Infantry in New Haven, Connecticut.

The regiment left for South Carolina in early 1864. It passed through Annapolis, where Newton had been three years before as a civilian attached to the Thirteenth New York. This time he wore a blue uniform. "I was in the full realization of what it meant to be again in the South, not a cringing black man, but a proud American soldier with the Union and Old Glory behind, before, over and under me."

His return to the South opened old wounds as he was reminded of injustices committed against him and others. "I confess that I had a burning desire to eke out some vengeance which for years had been pent up in my nature," he admitted. His better angels prevailed. "But, of course, from the Christian standpoint, this was all wrong. I was all wrong. I was then on a higher mission than trying to get personal vengeance on those who had mistreated me and mine. I was fighting for the liberty of my people and the righting of many wrongs that belonged to their social and religious welfare."

In the summer of 1864, the Twenty-ninth moved to Virginia and found itself on the front lines near Petersburg. Within days the regiment went into action at Deep Bottom, where Newton came close to death. "I remember a twenty-pound cannon ball coming towards me, I could see it distinctly through the smoke. It looked like it had been sent especially for me." He said a quick prayer. "When the ball was within about three feet of me it struck the ground and bounded over my head."

This was the first of many narrow escapes from death for Newton. Perhaps his closest call occurred on August 29. On that day he stood in the trenches, talking with his comrades, when an artillery shell struck the ground and exploded. It killed the private next to him. The force of the blast threw sand and dirt into Newton's face and temporarily blinded him. He never fully recovered his eyesight and later wore glasses.

About this time, he became a quartermaster sergeant and joined the regimental staff. He was serving in this capacity on April 3, 1865, when the Twenty-ninth numbered among the first Union forces to enter Richmond after Confederate troops withdrew. The next day, Abraham Lincoln visited the fallen Confederate capital. Newton noted, "We were present in Richmond when President Lincoln made his triumphal entry into the city. It was a sight never to be forgotten."

The Twenty-ninth left the Richmond area about two weeks later and, after a brief stint guarding prisoners at Point Lookout, Maryland, sailed for Texas. In October 1865, the regiment mustered out of service and returned to New Haven.

Newton rejoined his wife, Olivia, the daughter of *Weekly Anglo-African* newspaper editor Robert Hamilton, and his young daughter and son. He abandoned his profession as a mason and became a minister in the African Methodist Episcopal Church. After Olivia died, in 1868, he tended to the faithful at various places across the country. In Little Rock, Arkansas, he met a Sunday school secretary named Lulu Campbell. They married in 1876. Newton fathered another boy and girl with Lulu.

Newton rose to become an influential and respected church elder based in Camden, New Jersey. At the pinnacle of his career, personal tragedy devastated him. Over a six-year period beginning in 1899, he suffered the deaths of both of his daughters, his younger son, and his mother. He paid tribute to his family in a 1910 book, *Out of the Briars*. The title, he explained in the preface, is a metaphor that represents his emergence, torn and bleeding, from the thorns and briars of prejudice, hatred, and persecution of slavery.

Newton lived until age eighty-three, dying of heart problems in 1921.

In 2008, eighty-seven years after his death, families of the veterans in the Twenty-ninth dedicated a monument to the regiment in New Haven. It is composed of eight stone tablets marked with the names of those who served. The tablets surround an obelisk. Engraved on one face of it is a portrait of Newton and fellow quartermaster sergeant Daniel Lathrop taken from this carte de visite image. ⓖ

From *African American Faces of the Civil War: An Album of Union Soldiers and Their Stories* by Ronald S. Coddington, Copyright 2012 by The Johns Hopkins University Press. Reprinted by permission of the publisher.

THE ORIGIN OF
Memorial Day

Following the Civil War, the burden of death weighed heavily on the hearts of the American family. To find peace in such tragedy, those who lost a husband, son, or brother went to cemeteries to maintain their loved one's grave. This is the foundation of Memorial Day.

There is a long history of placing flowers at graves, but the Civil War made this upkeep a near-universal experience after an unprecedented number of lost soldiers. In 1868, three years after the war, a formal commemoration took place at Arlington National Cemetery. Future president James Garfield gave a speech before attendees decorated the 20,000 graves of Civil War soldiers, which soon became an annual tradition.

This holiday was originally called Decoration Day and only focused on those who were lost in the Civil War. However, after World War I, this observation soon became a time to honor all soldiers who died in an American war, and the name shifted to Memorial Day to reflect this development. In 1971, Congress passed an act that officially declared Memorial Day as a federal holiday.

For many in America, Memorial Day is an important time to remember and celebrate our loved ones who have passed. It is through this observation that the Civil War taught us an important lesson about how to deal with grief and find hope for the future.

> *We do not know one promise these men made, one pledge they gave, one word they spoke; but we do know they summed up and perfected, by one supreme act, the highest virtues of men and citizens. For love of country they accepted death, and thus resolved all doubts, and made immortal their patriotism and their virtue.*
>
> *—James A. Garfield, May 30, 1868*

AN INCIDENT OF GETTYSBURG—THE LAST THOUGHT OF A DYING FATHER.

The UNIDENTIFIED Father

Among the fallen at Gettysburg was an unknown soldier clutching a photograph of his children.

By Mark H. Dunkelman

The Humiston story inspired a flood of publicity, including this imaginary depiction of his famous death pose. It appeared in *Frank Leslie's Illustrated Newspaper.*

"**I** *got the likeness of the children,*" Amos Humiston wrote to his wife, Philinda, "and it pleased me more than anything that you could have sent me. How I want to see them and their mother is more than I can tell. I hope that we may all live to see each other again if this war does not last too long."

The likeness was an ambrotype — an early type of photograph — depicting 8-year-old Franklin, 6-year-old Alice and 4-year-old Frederick. Philinda had sent it from the Humistons' home in the western New York village of Portville to her husband in Virginia, where he was serving as a sergeant in Company C of the 154th New York Volunteer Infantry. The couple had no way of knowing that the picture would become the centerpiece of one of the most endearing and enduring human interest stories of the Battle of Gettysburg.

PHOTOS: MARK H. DUNKELMAN COLLECTION

The Humiston children, Frank, Fred and Alice, in a carte de visite copy of the ambrotype found in their dead father's hand. The image was produced in large quantities and many survive today.

When the unknown soldier was identified as Amos Humiston, his only portrait from life was retouched to add a beard and uniform and copies were sold to benefit his family.

Amos Humiston was 33 years old and had been a soldier for eight months when he received the ambrotype of his children. As a young man he had made a voyage of more than three years' duration aboard a whaling ship that carried him to exotic spots around the Pacific Ocean. On returning to his native Tioga County, New York, he met and fell in love with a young widow, Philinda Betsey Ensworth Smith. The two were married on Independence Day, 1854. By 1860 the couple and their three children were living in Portville, where Amos worked as a harness maker.

When the Civil War erupted, Amos "was anxious to enlist," Portville minister Isaac G. Ogden recalled, "but his duty to his family seemed then paramount to his duty to his country." While other men enlisted and left Cattaraugus County for the front, Amos remained at home with his wife and children and continued his labors in the harness shop.

When President Abraham Lincoln issued a call for 300,000 three-year volunteers in July 1862, Amos could no longer resist the urge to serve the Union cause. As Reverend Ogden recorded, when

Amos "received assurance from responsible citizens that his family should be cared for during his absence," he enlisted in good conscience. When another potential recruit hesitated, doubting his stamina to endure long marches, Amos encouraged him. "Come on," he told the young man. "I will carry your musket for you."

Letters to Home

From the 154th Regiment's rendezvous at Jamestown, New York, Amos sent the first of a series of letters to Philinda. He reported he had a cold and complained about the camp's food. Then he touched on themes he would repeat throughout his correspondence: His love for his family, how much he missed them, and his concern for their welfare. "It will not do for me to say that I would like to see you," he informed Philinda. "They would say that I was homesick." He added a message for little Frank, Alice and Fred: "Tell the babies that I want to see them very much."

After mustering into the service in late September 1862, the 154th New York was shipped by rail to Washington, D.C. and joined the Army of the Potomac's 11th Corps in northern Virginia. "The prospect is that we shall have a fight before long," Amos informed Philinda in an early letter from the front. "The sooner the better."

However, the first seven months of the regiment's service was spent becoming accustomed to army life and making inconsequential marches from camp to camp. When Amos became ill he told Philinda, "I can die in battle like a man, but I hate the idea of dying here like a hog." On recovering he resumed his typical good cheer. As usual, his letters were filled with expressions of love for his family. He fantasized about being home for the holidays, kissing Philinda's red cheeks and having the children prattle as he held them on his knees. "Rest assured there is no being on earth that wants to see you half as much as I do," he guaranteed Philinda. "Tell them babies that Pa wants to see them very much."

When his Christmas and New Year's dinners turned out to be hardtack and salt pork, he wished he could visit Philinda's pantry. He also had other pleasures in mind. "If I ever live to get home," he told his wife, "you will not complain about being lonesome again or of sleeping cold for I will lay as close to you as the bark to a tree." Over and over he asked her to kiss the children for him.

In March 1863, after recovering from a bout of diarrhea, he sent Philinda a special composition he described as "some of the crazy productions of my brain in the shape of poetry." His verses imagined the children dreaming of him while he dreamed of home during lonely picket duty. "Oh when will this rebellion cease," he wondered, "This cursed war be o'er/And we our dear ones meet/To part from them no more?"

On to Gettysburg

In May 1863 the 154th New York suffered heavy losses in its first battle, Chancellorsville. Amos had a close call when a spent bullet struck a glancing blow over his heart. It "made me think of home," he wrote. Back in camp when the

"If I ever live to get home, you will not complain about being lonesome again or of sleeping cold for I will lay as close to you as the bark to a tree."

campaign closed, he received the ambrotype of his beloved children. He carried it with him thereafter, as the regiment made the long march through northern Virginia and Maryland to Gettysburg.

On July 1 the 154th New York was rushed from Gettysburg's Cemetery Hill through the village to John Kuhn's brickyard in the northeastern outskirts of the village. The regiment and two others of its brigade attempted to cover the retreat of other 11th Corps units. Opposed by two Confederate brigades and outnumbered by more than three to one, the Union soldiers were powerless to offer more than token resistance. Much of the 154th was surrounded and forced to surrender. A few men managed to escape and race back to the shelter of Cemetery Hill.

Identifying Amos

After the battle, among the many corpses was one of a Union soldier clutching an ambrotype of his three children. There was nothing on his person to identify him. A doctor from Philadelphia, John Francis Bourns, who came to Gettysburg to help tend the thousands of wounded in the aftermath of the battle, realized the ambrotype was the single, sad clue to the identity of the soldier and his family. Bourns took the picture home with him to Philadelphia and instigated a wave of publicity about the incident in the press. Newspaper after newspaper throughout the North ran articles summarizing the circumstances and minutely describing the image. "Whose Father Was He?" read the headline of one widely reprinted story. Bourns simultaneously had hundreds of copies of the ambrotype made as small, cardboard-mounted cartes de visite photographs to be sent to inquirers.

A month after the first article appeared, the *American Presbyterian*, a religious journal published in Philadelphia, announced, "The Dead Soldier Identified." A copy of that paper containing a description of the ambrotype had reached Philinda Humiston's hands. She had obtained a carte de visite from Dr. Bourns and on seeing it realized that she was a widow and her three children were fatherless.

A second great wave of publicity swept the North, announcing the identity of the devoted father. The touching incident inspired the creation of prose, poetry and songs. Proceeds from the sale of the children's image and that of Amos went to succor the bereaved family.

Dr. Bourns, realizing the impact the incident had made on the public, used it as the catalyst for the founding of the Homestead, an orphanage for soldiers' children in Gettysburg. Philinda and the children moved to the Homestead for a period in the postwar years. Unfortunately, after a decade of service, the Homestead — the great good inspired by the Humiston family's tragedy — met its own melodramatic end when its matron was charged with cruelty to the orphans, and Bourns was accused of embezzling money meant for them.

Amos Humistons' Legacy

The Humistons spent the rest of their lives downplaying the incident that had made them famous. Philinda remarried and eventually buried her third husband. Frank became a beloved doctor in Jaffrey, New Hampshire. Fred became a traveling salesman out of Boston. Both men married and had children. Alice never married and lived a nomadic life, eventually settling in Glendale, California, where she died in 1933 after suffering burns in an accident. She is buried there; her mother and two brothers are buried in Jaffrey.

Amos Humiston died young, as had his father and grandfather. Premature death struck three succeeding generations, a factor in keeping the family small. The eight grandchildren of Amos and Philinda produced only seven great-grandchildren, who in turn had a dozen great-great-grandchildren. There are at least ten great-great-great-grandchildren, making for approximately a score of living Humiston descendants scattered from Maine to the Yukon.

Several of them were on hand in 1993 when a monument to Amos was erected and dedicated on North Stratton Street in Gettysburg, marking the approximate spot where he was found grasping the ambrotype. It is the only monument to an individual enlisted man on the battlefield. **G**

Mark H. Dunkelman is the author of Gettysburg's Unknown Soldier: The Life, Death, and Celebrity of Amos Humiston *and four other books on the Civil War.*

Inspired by the Amos Humiston story, the Homestead orphanage opened on Baltimore Street in Gettysburg in 1866 and operated for 11 years before it shut down amid scandal. Among the first occupants were Philinda Humiston and her three children.

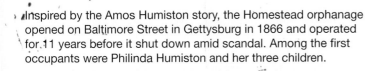

The Art

of

Reenactors tote muskets — and paintbrushes or banjos, too.

By Lucas Bernhardt

Last fall, artist Henry Kidd was out photographing the battlefield at Gettysburg, finding backgrounds he would later fill with charging and wounded soldiers in his paintings. He stopped at a gift shop where a framed reliquary containing bullets and other wartime artifacts caught his eye. Above the case was a photograph of the famed Confederate Gen. Lewis Armistead. On closer inspection, Kidd realized it was a photograph of himself playing Armistead at a Civil War reenactment.

"We take these things pretty seriously," says Kidd, who has been participating in reenactments for over 25 years.

War

Union soldiers charge the Confederate line at the 150th anniversary reenactment of the First Battle of Bull Run in July 2011.

Authenticity is Key

Like many who regularly participate in these events, Kidd devotes a great deal of time, energy and creativity to bringing the Civil War to life. "I try to do it with as much detail as possible," he says, which means wearing an authentic uniform and researching his impression extensively, even going so far as to work with the Museum of the Confederacy to learn the rebel yell that Confederate soldiers used in combat. It also means remaining in character throughout the battle, and sometimes beyond.

He recalls marching a full 63 miles to reenact at the 125th anniversary of the battle and surrender at Appomattox. Afterward his troop marched into a field where they were met by a disbanded unit of the Union Army. "All of us stayed in first person," he says. "I remember walking up to someone and saying, 'Hey Yank, you got anything to eat?'" What followed was a heartfelt exchange of food and souvenirs, uniform buttons and scraps of their respective flags.

Kidd explains that he makes art about the Civil War and reenacts battles for the same reason: "To commemorate the bravery and sacrifice of these men, and to tell their stories so future generations won't forget them. We don't know how

Artist and reenactor Henry Kidd poses as Confederate Gen. Lewis Armistead.

PHOTOS BY HENRY KIDD

many great authors, how many great artists, poets, actors and painters were killed in their prime, and we don't know what they could have done for humanity."

Family Matters

This lesson was made more personal for him when he reenacted Pickett's Charge with his son during the 135th anniversary of Gettysburg. "It was the largest reenactment I have ever been to. There were 26,000 reenactors there. We had 1,500 more men going into Pickett's Charge than General Pickett had," he says. Both Kidd and his son were privates in the battle, and their unit drew straws to determine injuries and where each soldier would fall. Kidd was one of the lucky few who would cross the stone wall, but his son went down in the field with a leg wound.

"He grabbed his leg," says Kidd, "and he looked back at me and said, 'I'm okay dad.' I had to keep going, and the fellow marching beside me put his hand on my shoulder and said, 'He's in the Lord's hands now.'"

In a flash, Kidd understood that this was something that really happened – that fathers and sons had gone into battle together and been separated by fate. "There are moments at the reenactments when everything modern around us is gone, and we really, oddly feel that we're feeling what it must have been like," he says.

Another memorable moment for Kidd happened during a reenactment of the Battle of Spotsylvania. As his unit was retaking a line of breastworks, he encountered a lone Union soldier standing among his fallen comrades. "Nothing was wrong with him," Kidd says. "He was just sitting there holding his musket with a very serious look on his face." Kidd reached across the breastworks, put a hand on the man's shoulder, and said, "Come on over, Billy, you're captured."

The man burst into tears and said, "Thank you. I was praying some rebel would come and tell me I was captured. My great-grandfather was captured at this spot during the war."

As someone with ancestors who were in Robert E. Lee's army, Kidd could relate. "It is a family matter with me," he says. "I know my great-grand-

The Union line advances during a reenactment of the Battle of Cedar Creek in Middletown, Virginia.

GIVE IT A TRY

If you're interested in taking part in a civil war reenactment, reenactor Henry Kidd suggests finding a unit in your area and getting a feel for its routine. Many units have equipment you can borrow and also offer training. "I don't think you'll regret it," he says.

While some units don't allow women, over the past 15 years the reenactment community has seen an increase in participation by women, either as living historians at camp or as soldiers. "There were women who went into the war disguised as men," Kidd says. "I think the groups that frown on women are missing a lot. They add so much to our impression."

father lost his brother in hand-to-hand fighting on South Mountain. So I think about them. North or South, they need to be remembered."

Kidd designed the banners and logos for both of the major reenactment events for the Battle of Gettysburg's 150th anniversary. One takes place July 4 to 7 and is hosted by the Gettysburg Anniversary Committee, a community organization that stages yearly reenactments at Gettysburg. The other takes place June 27 to 30 and is put on by the Blue Gray Alliance, a nonprofit supported by many of the larger reenacting organizations.

Kidd has agreed to be the official artist for the Blue Gray Alliance event, and has created a new series of paintings in its honor. He will be dividing his time between the artist's booth and the battlefield. "My heart is torn," he says, "but I'll be on the field whenever they're fighting."

"...this was something that really happened — that fathers and sons had gone into battle together and been separated by fate."

In this, Kidd may be the exception. Many of the artists and artisans at reenactments stay in the sutler or the civilian areas of the events.

Music and Muskets

Traditionally, sutlers supplied food and clothing to the army, but at reenactments they serve and entertain all comers. There, among craftsmen and storytellers, you can hear period music played by groups like the 2nd South Carolina String Band.

"We perform in a historical setting and in a historical context," says Joe Ewers, the band's banjo player. "We take pains to educate people about where the music came from and what the songs are about. The lyrics to some of these songs do afford the twentieth-century person a glimpse into what life was like on the farm, on the plantation, on the river and in the cities during those times."

The band formed organically in the late 1980s among a group of reenactors from Massachusetts who would play music around the campfire after events. The members had all learned songs like "Oh Susanna" and "Camptown Races" in grade school. The playing came easily and was widely appreciated. "We used to draw pretty large crowds, but you couldn't tell because it was dark," Ewers says. "You'd take a break and walk around, and suddenly you'd see that there were hundreds of people around your camp."

By the mid-1990s they had done their homework and had a better sense of the instruments, playing styles and songs that were popular among soldiers in the Civil War. They discovered that while parlor music had a strong following on the homefront, soldiers tended to prefer the music of the minstrel stage. But for the band it wasn't as easy as just digging through books and sheet music to find the songs that soldiers actually played. "There's a whole lot of Civil War music, but there isn't a lot of really good Civil War music," Ewers says.

The band also had to confront the reality that many minstrel songs would be offensive to contemporary audiences. "We got rid of as much of

The 150th anniversary reenactment of the First Battle of Bull Run.

HENRY KIDD

the insensitive language as possible," Ewers says, noting that favoring authenticity to the point that it alienates audience members "doesn't bring anything to the party at all."

For a decade, band members would clock out of work Friday, drive from Massachusetts down to Pennsylvania, Maryland or beyond, then pitch their tents and catch a few hours of sleep. The next day they would be up early to run drills from nineteenth-century military manuals. In the afternoon they went to war, and then they played music late into the night. Sundays meant another battle before packing up and making the long trip home.

"We stopped toting the musket in 2000," Ewers says, but the band is still drawn to the excitement and camaraderie of the reenactments. At dances and around campfires their music remains in demand. **G**

HAYK SHALUNTS / SHUTTERSTOCK.COM

The 2nd South Carolina String Band is composed of reenactors from Massachusetts.

2ND SOUTH CAROLINA STRING BAND

i

For more information about reenactments and additional Civil War–related events in Gettysburg or in your area, visit www.milsurpia.com/events/civil-war-reenactments

Saving the Battlefield

Gettysburg today reflects the labor of thousands and a fundamental shift in preservation philosophy.

By Lucas Bernhardt

The Battle of Gettysburg transformed an out-of-the-way college town into an important symbol of America. But the battle over what this symbol means and how it should be preserved has taken many forms over the years.

Preservation efforts began at roughly the same time that the Civil War ended. At Abraham Lincoln's request, a group of Gettysburg businessmen set about buying battlefield land. Tourists began arriving to mourn the dead. And just as quickly, tourism came to dominate the local economy.

By the mid-1880s, early preservationists formed the Gettysburg Battlefield Memorial Association. With their support, the first authoritative history of the battle was published and efforts were made to map the entire battlefield.

Tourism in Gettysburg

At this time, a new rail line into Gettysburg magnified the already vibrant tourist trade, and a new crop of hotels and retailers sprung up around town. For this second generation of tourists, visiting the battlefield was as much about patriotic feeling as it was about mourning fallen soldiers.

With the rise of the automobile, Gettysburg's tourist amenities spread and replaced farms along the roads into town. During the Great Depression, the National Park Service took over the administration of the battlefield. Tourism dipped, but the Civilian Conservation Corps and Works Progress Administration (WPA) workers were busy improving the park's infrastructure and building a comfort station, a ranger station and various other facilities.

Throughout the twentieth century, Gettysburg National Military Park saw near constant additions: parking lots, monuments, memorials, paved trails, cannons and ever-expanding facilities. The idea was to attract as many visitors as possible. The town of Gettysburg kept pace, building right up to the edge of the battlefield: eateries, souvenir shops, even a wax museum.

Then, in 1999, the tide turned.

Focus on Restoration

Going into the new century, the Park Service shifted its focus from developing the battlefield to restoring it. The Park Service's 1999 management plan stated that "because natural systems are not static but dynamic, re-creating and perpetuating the stage upon which real events took place requires a particularly sensitive and carefully coordinated natural resource management effort." In other words, it's a lot of work keeping Gettysburg the way it was.

The implosion in 2000 of Gettysburg National Tower, an observation deck adjacent to the battlefield, was the start of a big change. Since then, the Park Service has gone to extraordinary lengths to recapture the past, razing nonhistoric buildings, reducing the white-tailed deer population to one-fifteenth its former size, clearing forests in order to restore historical farms and orchards and reintroducing thousands of native plants.

Motivating the National Park Service is a belief that without seeing the original landscape, visitors cannot fully understand the Battle of Gettysburg. But the park service efforts have brought collateral benefits. In researching soldiers' use of land, the park service discovered that the battle, despite its size and many unexpected turns, was fought almost entirely by the book. According to a National Park Service press release, "General Meade would have received an 'A' from his instructors at West Point for his application of terrain analysis principles during this, his greatest practical exercise."

Park service restoration efforts have also benefited the environment by reintroducing grasslands and wetlands. "The park has been identified by the Audubon Society as an important bird area and an important mammal area because of its grasslands habitat — one of the most threatened habitats in Pennsylvania," says ranger Katie Lawhon.

For Lawhon, preserving the battlefield helps to keep the memory of the battle alive. "I believe it is the story of the battle, and in particular the aftermath and Lincoln's Gettysburg Address, that gives Gettysburg so much meaning and importance to Americans today," she says. And she admits that after 18 years of working at the park, she still gets choked up telling the story.

It turns out that keeping a 6,000-acre park frozen in time is no small task. Along with over 100 employees, Gettysburg National Military Park has enlisted an army of nearly 3,000 volunteers to keep the place orderly and historically accurate. That's

...after 18 years of working at the park, [Ranger Katie Lawhon] still gets choked up telling the story.

approximately two-and-a-half volunteers for every monument and memorial in the park.

The Growing Scope of Preservation

While efforts to improve the main battlefield continue — for example, by replicating fences that were up in 1863 — the more heated preservation battles have moved out to the flanks. The Civil War Trust, the nation's largest nonprofit organization dedicated to preserving Civil War battlefields, is engaged in ongoing efforts to purchase and rehabilitate land where more obscure battles and troop movements took place.

"We work closely with the National Park Service, and frequently rely on their priority list for preservation," says Jim Campi, director of policy and communications at the trust. "Our goal is to preserve the battlefields and to protect them from the sprawl that's enveloping so many of them."

In recent years that has meant both acquiring land near battlefields and organizing grassroots campaigns to oppose inappropriate construction near historical sites. Although it has preserved 900 acres around Gettysburg, the Civil War Trust is better known in the area for having prevented the construction of two casinos. Locals, history buffs and Civil War reenactors keep the nonprofit informed when new development plans are in the works and when a historically significant property goes up for sale.

The Civil War Trust is currently waging "The Forgotten Flanks of Gettysburg" campaign, raising grant money and donations to save another 112 acres at the far corners of the battlefield. "There's always going to be debate about the meaning of these places," Campi says. "Our perspective is, let's focus on preserving them so you can have that debate."

Ⓖ

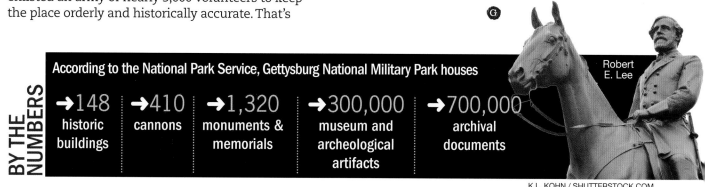

BY THE NUMBERS

According to the National Park Service, Gettysburg National Military Park houses

→148 historic buildings | →410 cannons | →1,320 monuments & memorials | →300,000 museum and archeological artifacts | →700,000 archival documents

Robert E. Lee

K.L. KOHN / SHUTTERSTOCK.COM

Monuments at Gettysburg are everywhere. By the side of the road, in the middle of a carefully preserved portion of the battlefield, or within sight of commercial buildings. Some stand alone, but many are grouped together as tight comrades. Visitors seek out large and striking monuments as well as the humble monuments that mark the spots where regiments fought amidst unimaginable din and smoke and suffering.

Monumental Fields

Gettysburg is home to over a thousand reminders of loss and valor.

By Ben Nussbaum
photos by Tom Eishen, GettysburgPhotographs.com

In 1998, this statue honoring Confederate Lt. Gen. James Longstreet, the leader of the 1st Corps, was erected. It is one of more than 1,300 monuments and memorials at Gettysburg National Military Park.

The collection of granite and bronze grew slowly. The first monument at Gettysburg, the 1st Minnesota Memorial Urn, lies inside Gettysburg National Cemetery. It was erected in 1867 by the regiment's survivors. More than a decade passed before another monument was built.

Triggered by the 25th anniversary of the battle, the building boom began. Many monuments were paid for by surviving members of the regiments they honor, but Northern states also paid for additional memorials or allocated money to supplement the money raised by veterans. In the twentieth century, Southern states also erected monuments at Gettysburg. Construction of new memorials has slowed but continues, with monuments to Lt. Gen. James Longstreet and Abraham Lincoln added in 1998 and 2009, respectively.

Virginia State Memorial

In 1917, Virginia became the first Southern state to erect a monument, setting the template for other former Confederate states to build large shrines along Seminary Ridge.

The Virginia State Memorial features a noble Robert E. Lee on horseback atop a column. At the base of the column, seven soldiers, the detritus of battle at their feet, contrast with the poised Lee. According to the memorial, "[t]he group represents various types who left civil occupations to join the Confederate Army. … a professional man, a mechanic, an artist, a boy, a business man, a farmer, a youth."

Virginia contributed over 19,000 men to the Army of Northern Virginia at Gettysburg, the most of any Southern state. It is fitting that the Virginia memorial was the first and is the largest of the Southern memorials.

VIRGINIA TO HER SONS AT GETTYSBURG

High Water Mark of the Confederacy

North Carolina State Memorial

In the years after 1863, both the Battle of Gettysburg and, more specifically, Pickett's Charge were considered the farthest line of advance of the Confederacy. The High Water Mark of the Confederacy monument is placed in front of the Copse of Trees, the battlefield landmark that the Confederates used to guide their march during the ill-fated charge. It depicts a book, on whose pages are written the Confederate and Union units that fought during the charge.

The monument captures some of the postwar history of the battlefield. The Gettysburg Battlefield Memorial Association (GBMA) managed the area for the first several decades after the war. It set the initial standards for where monuments could be located and what they could look like. This monument, conceived by the GBMA and listing on its back the names of the directors of the GBMA, was completed in 1895, the same year that the association transferred control of the battlefield and the 320 monuments it then contained to the federal government.

The North Carolina State Memorial was sculpted by Gutzon Borglum, who is most famous for carving Mount Rushmore. It depicts a group of soldiers as they start across the fields to participate in Pickett's Charge. The memorial is situated so that it appears as if the soldiers have just come through the trees and are now looking at the vast expanse of space they must cover under fire before encountering the Union Army.

The faces of the men are modeled on photographs of Confederate veterans; the color bearer is modeled after Orren Randolph Smith, who designed the Confederate national flag.

Brig. Gen. Gouverneur Warren Statue

Warren, the Chief Engineer of the Army of the Potomac, stood atop Little Round Top on July 2 and surveyed the field. Joining him on the otherwise undefended outcrop were a few signalmen who were packing up, preparing to leave the spot.

In the distance, Warren spotted Confederate battlelines. He ordered the signalmen to stay to create the illusion that the location was defended. He rushed to secure troops to defend the hill, earning himself the title "Savior of Little Round Top."

The statue is perched at the summit of Little Round Top, with Warren forever scanning the fields of battle.

1ˢᵗ Minnesota Infantry

On the second day of fighting, the Confederate Army swept through Maj. Gen. Daniel Sickles' 3rd Corps at the Peach Orchard and moved toward an exposed position along Cemetery Ridge. Union commanders frantically attempted to bring in artillery to defend the position and provide shelter for the many Union wounded.

To delay the Confederate onslaught, 262 men from the 1st Minnesota charged into the low ground in front of the present memorial. Behind them the Union line along Cemetery Ridge reformed. The 1st Minnesota had done its job, but 215 of its soldiers were dead or wounded. The regiment's survivors fought the next day on the Union line during Pickett's Charge; another 17 men were lost.

The first memorial at Gettysburg, a simple urn in the Soldiers' National Cemetery, was built by the survivors of the 1st Minnesota in 1867. In 1893, the state of Minnesota erected this tribute. The soldier atop the base charges forward at double quick pace.

90th Pennsylvania Infantry

Three monuments at Gettysburg pay tribute to the 90th Pennsylvania. The regiment's survivors paid for a traditional monument in Ziegler's Grove, showing an eagle perched atop a drum that tops a granite shaft. The Commonwealth of Pennsylvania paid for the other two monuments — a large position marker on Hancock Avenue and the Granite Tree Monument, perhaps the most distinctive monument on the battlefield.

Located on Oak Hill, the monument represents a tree battered by battle. From the tree hang recognizable tokens of a soldier's life — a canteen, a rifle, a cartridge bag — along with a shield and other symbolic items. On a stump of branch at the top of the tree a bird's nest holds a mother bird and her babies. An often-repeated story recounts how a soldier of the 90th risked his life to return a nest that had been knocked from a tree due to the violence of battle.

The tree, for all its whimsy, is a monument to terrible losses. The monument's plaque reads, in part: "On the afternoon of July 1, 1863, killed and mortally wounded 11, wounded 44, captured or missing 39, total 94, of 208."

Pennsylvania State Memorial
The most expensive memorial, it includes the names of over 34,000 Pennsylvanians who fought at Gettysburg.

20th Massachusetts Infantry
The 30-ton boulder is puddingstone, a type of rock formation found in and near Boston. The monument came about because several of the men in the regiment remembered climbing on such boulders when they were boys.

John Burns Statue

John Burns was the only civilian to fight at Gettysburg. A veteran of the War of 1812, he arrived on the battlefield on July 1 in a peculiar outfit. According to Maj. Thomas Chamberlain, it "consisted of dark trousers and a waistcoat, a blue 'swallow tail' coat with burnished brass buttons, such as used to be affected by well-to-do gentlemen of the old school about 40 years ago, and a high black silk hat, from which most of the original gloss had long departed, of a shape to be found only in the fashion plates of the remote past." He was toting a flintlock musket and powder horn, although he soon borrowed a modern rifle.

He surprised the soldiers by fighting with them bravely and coolly. Wounded in three places and unable to retreat, he was found by the Confederates but convinced them that he was a noncombatant.

Burns become a national celebrity, his fame stoked by a poem by Bret Harte that reads, in part,

The only man who didn't back down
When the rebels rode through his native town;
But held his own in the fight next day,
When all his townsfolk ran away.

… Burns, unmindful of jeer and scoff,
Stood there picking the rebels off,—
With his long brown rifle, and bell-crowned hat,
And the swallow-tails they were laughing at.

73rd New York Infantry

The 73rd New York was composed mainly of volunteer firefighters in New York City. The monument depicts two men — one dressed as a firefighter, one a soldier.

Part of the Excelsior Brigade, the 73rd fought in the Peach Orchard on Gettysburg's second day, suffering severe casualties. Their leader that day, Maj. Henry Tremain, told his fellow veterans the following at the monument's dedication in 1887: "By common consent this battlefield is to represent the fields of four years of war. These monuments at one battlefield are to represent all battlefields where [soldiers] engaged in other battles against a common enemy and upheld a common cause. These monuments typify a world of history, a multitude of lives and a multitude of deaths."

20th Maine Infantry

This monument on Little Round Top commemorates a regiment made famous by the book *The Killer Angels* by Michael Shaara and the movie based on it, *Gettysburg*. The regiment, out of ammunition, charged down the slope to capture and scatter stunned Confederates, thus protecting the far left of the Union line.

7th New Jersey Infantry

This eye-catching monument depicts a Minié ball, the standard bullet of the Civil War.

Going to Gettysburg

The historic town and sprawling park welcome visitors.

By Roger Morris

The countryside surrounding the town of Gettysburg is the perfect theater for a battle between armies of tens of thousands of foot soldiers, dashing horse cavalry units and huge, relentlessly pounding artillery batteries of small but deadly cannons. The area is still primarily rolling farmland 150 years later. Visitors can see miles across pastures and meadows. It is easy to picture thousands of soldiers taking cover on and behind a range of small, rounded hills while snipers rained fire from the many stretches of woodland or from behind the small boulders that litter the area.

Gettysburg itself still resembles a typical college town — which it is — of small brick-and-clapboard houses and shops. Fleeing soldiers, wounded and exhausted, were pursued by onrushing cavalry through this warren of small streets.

Visitors Can Go Back in Time

The battlefield remains largely as it was, although a small part of it has been built upon at the edge of town. A 24-mile, self-guided auto route through the battlefield is the main attraction. There is also a marvelous and comprehensive visitor center, a military cemetery where many of the Union dead are buried, the house where President Abraham Lincoln polished his famous address delivered four months after the battle and, of course, the town itself. Although there are souvenir shops in town, Gettysburg has little of the tackiness of many historic areas. There are plenty of places to stay, from quaint B&Bs to upscale hotels, and the usual range of places to eat.

How can a visitor best take in all the offerings at Gettysburg? It depends largely on what you want, how flexible your schedule is, and whether you are traveling by yourself or with family or friends.

If you want to get a sense of the horrible battle that took place a century and a half ago, two to four hours — the amount of time for the automobile tour — is enough. But if you want to understand how it happened — how the battle unfolded in stages over the three days, its ebbs and flows, the strategies of Union Gen. George G. Meade and Confederate Gen. Robert E. Lee and what their troops did, or didn't do, then allow a day, possibly two.

Either way, start at the visitor center, a large, modern building with a base of native stone that sits isolated on the southern part of town, situated among surrounding woods. It is on the edge of the main battlefield, which primarily abuts the town of Gettysburg's western border.

There is no admission charge to the center or for the auto tour through the battlefield. At the center you can make final decisions on what to do. There is a restaurant to grab a snack, a marvelous bookstore and gift shop, a state-of-the-art museum, and two featured attractions: a 20-minute film, *A New Birth of Freedom*, narrated by Morgan Freeman, and a cyclorama depicting Pickett's Charge, the turning point of the battle. A small admission fee covers the movie, cyclorama, and museum. These are nice, especially as an orientation for children.

The Auto Tour

You can hire a licensed guide or board a tour bus, but the battlefield is easy to navigate and understand by yourself. An excellent map and foldout guide is free. You can also buy a detailed guide at the bookstore, similar to headset tours you can get at other museums. This will take you around the battlefield in under three hours.

The tour first leads you briefly through town to where the battle began just to the northwest. The rest of the loop is on well-marked one- or two-lane roads. Most of the 16 planned stops have slots for parallel parking on the road itself. Other stops have parking lots and let you explore a bit, plus there are a handful of elevated observation points and towers.

But you are not permitted to roam the battlefield at will, and there are multiple signs warning "No Relic Hunting," which indicates how much debris from the battle exists even after all these years.

i

HOURS

Gettysburg National Military Park is open daily from 30 minutes before sunrise to 30 minutes after sunset. The museum and visitor center are open daily (except on Thanksgiving, Christmas and New Year's Day) from 9 a.m. to 4 p.m. from December 1 through February 28 and 8 a.m. to 5 p.m. from March 1 through October 31. Entry to the park is free. Tickets give you access to museum exhibits, *A New Birth of Freedom* film and the cyclorama. Information: www.nps.gov/gett/

APPRECIATING THE CYCLORAMA

Gettysburg's cyclorama is a massive painting displayed so that it forms a circle; viewers stand in the middle and are literally surrounded by the depiction of Pickett's Charge. Gettysburg's cyclorama is historic in three ways:

First, it illustrates Pickett's Charge in a mostly accurate, if romanticized, way. French painter Paul Philippoteaux spent several weeks on the battlefield in 1882, making sketches of the local terrain. He also talked with numerous veterans of the battle and enlisted a local photographer to create panoramic reference photographs.

Second, it is one of the lone survivors of what was once a popular form of storytelling. In the late 1800s, many hundreds, if not thousands, of these huge paintings were produced. Special buildings were erected in major cities to house them, and cycloramas would travel to state fairs and other locations around the country. Only about 30 cycloramas still survive; of those, only four are in the United States, and only three, including the one at Gettysburg, are viewable.

And third, Gettysburg's cyclorama has a long history at Gettysburg. It was originally created to be displayed in Boston, where it was exhibited for almost 20 years. It was reconstructed at Gettysburg in time for the 50th anniversary of the battle in 1913. It has been on display at Gettysburg, except for periods when it was being renovated, more or less continuously for 100 years.

The memorials are constantly present roadside. Many fields are ringed by stone walls and split-rail fences, and there are sweeping vistas with the Appalachian foothills in the distance.

Most of the tour focuses on the second and third days of fighting, first through the western hills where the Confederates massed and then the eastern hills at the edge of town where the Union forces took up mainly defensive positions against the charges that came across the open fields in between. The final stop is the Soldiers' National Cemetery, where Union dead are buried and where Lincoln gave his address.

The visitor center and the battleground tour can be completed in two to four hours, although traffic can be slow on busy days. To better understand the events of 150 years ago, visit the center and drive the battleground in an afternoon. Then spend the evening in town. That night look through the map and guidebook, matching what you read with what you saw. Return the next morning for a final drive through.

For those who prefer others means of exploration, there are biking, horseback and some walking opportunities. Biking is permitted on the same route as the auto tour, but no biking is allowed off-road or on trails. The main parking lot and some tour stops have bike racks. The park has bridle paths, but you must either bring your own horse (van-parking facilities are very limited) or rent one at private concessions near the park. A self-guided walking tour of the cemetery is available, as are some ranger-led walking programs. Camping is available in the park, but only for the Boy Scouts and other youth groups and on a reservation basis. Picnicking is permitted at the visitor center and at Warfield Ridge, midway through the auto tour. **G**

Many battlefields and historic sites are within a short drive of Gettysburg.

By Dean Sagar

Antietam, Maryland

Beyond Gettysburg

The Gettysburg campaign was the largest of three Confederate invasions of the North, one in each year from 1862 to 1864. The three campaigns shared common goals: to spread discontent and opposition to the war, disrupt vital railroad and telegraph communications, and replenish stores of food, horses and supplies from the bountiful farms of Maryland and Pennsylvania.

The area around Gettysburg is thick with battlefields and historic towns and cities. Antietam is well-known and, like Gettysburg, memorialized with a national battlefield park. Other historic sites are preserved as parts of state parks and local historic districts, while some are remembered through local historical societies.

1. Antietam, Maryland

Following his victory at Second Bull Run in August 1862, Gen. Robert E. Lee ordered his army of 55,000 men into Maryland to obtain badly needed horses and supplies, hoping that winning a victory on Northern soil might gain recognition for the Confederacy from Britain and France. Alerted to Lee's plans by a mislaid dispatch, Gen. George McClellan mobilized his 75,000-man Army of the Potomac to block Lee's advance. At dawn on September 17, McClellan launched an attack against Lee's troops, which were waiting in defensive

Gettysburg **77**

positions behind Antietam Creek near the town of Sharpsburg.

Throughout the day the two armies attacked and counterattacked through cornfields and around a Dunker church until Federal troops were able to overwhelm the Confederates along a sunken road at the center of the Confederate line. Rather than follow up on this success, McClellan hesitated while his reserve under Gen. Ambrose Burnside attacked a Confederate position defending a stone arch bridge across the creek. A stubborn defense by 500 Georgians succeeded in holding off the Union attack for three hours, allowing time for Gen. A.P. Hill's division to arrive and launch a counterattack that ended the battle in a stalemate. At day's end, some 23,000 men were dead, wounded or missing in what was the bloodiest single day of the entire war.

The sunken road, stone arch bridge (now Burnside Bridge) and restored Dunker church are preserved as part of the 3,200-acre Antietam National Battlefield Park, located ten miles south of I-70. The park features an 8.5-mile self-guided tour of the battlefield, which has over 90 monuments. The park's visitor center offers a 26-minute orientation film, battlefield exhibits and daily lectures.

➔ Visitors may also want to tour the adjoining Antietam National Cemetery (www.nps.gov/anti/historyculture/antietam-national-cemetery.htm), the Pry House Field Hospital Museum (www.nps.gov/anti/planyourvisit/pryhouse.htm) and the town of Sharpsburg, which served as a Confederate rear base and hospital during the battle. Sharpsburg's historic district is architecturally significant for its impressive number of preserved Georgian-inspired stone houses and the early Federal-style brick buildings lining the town square.

HOURS

Antietam National Battlefield is open during daylight hours except for Thanksgiving, Christmas and New Year's Day. The visitor center is open daily from 9 a.m. to 4 p.m.

INFORMATION

www.nps.gov/anti

2. Monocacy Junction, Maryland

In July 1864, a Confederate force under Gen. Jubal Early and former U.S. Vice President Gen. John C. Breckinridge marched into Maryland with instructions from Lee to menace the northern defenses of Washington in the hope of drawing forces away from the sizeable Union Army threatening Richmond. The Confederates marched unopposed as far north as Hagerstown, Maryland, then moved southeast through Frederick toward Washington. An advance force under Breckinridge and Gen. John B. Gordon found their route blocked by a hastily assembled Union force under Gen. Lew Wallace on the east side of Monocacy River. Attacking across the river and an open wheatfield, the Confederates overcame stiff resistance from three Federal lines in what Gordon described as "one of the severest [battles] ever fought" by his troops. Gordon lost nearly a third of his command in the attack, with both sides losing over 2,360 dead and wounded in an hour of intense fighting.

The Union defense at Monocacy delayed the Confederate march on

HOURS

Monocacy National Battlefield is open Monday through Friday from 7:30 a.m. to sunset and Saturday and Sunday from 8:30 a.m. to sunset, except Thanksgiving, Christmas and New Year's Day. The visitor center is open Thursday through Monday from 9 a.m. to 5 p.m.

INFORMATION

www.nps.gov/mono/index

Washington by a day, allowing time for Gen. Ulysses S. Grant to transport thousands of troops up the Potomac River to reinforce Washington's defenses.

Portions of the Monocacy site are now a National Battlefield Park with a small visitor center that includes an interpretive battlefield map, multimedia exhibits and a bookstore. There are park ranger programs and occasional weekend reenactments of Union battle drills. Self-guided driving and walking tours direct visitors to several restored farmhouses that played important roles in the battle and five commemorative monuments, including a large memorial honoring the 14th New Jersey Regiment, which lost two-thirds of its men in the fight.

ZACK FRANK / SHUTTERSTOCK.COM

➜ Visitors may also want to tour a number of Civil War sites in nearby Frederick, including the National Museum of Civil War Medicine (www.civilwarmed. org) and the restored Barbara Fritchie House Museum (barbarafritchie.org). Frederick's downtown historic district has over 40 square blocks of unique shops, galleries and restaurants and is considered one of the prime antique centers in the Mid-Atlantic.

3. Williamsport, Maryland

After the battle at Gettysburg, Lee ordered the main part of his army to retreat to Virginia, retracing its earlier path to Williamsport on the Potomac River. Through continuous rain, a wagon caravan carrying almost 10,000 Confederate wounded slowly made its way to Williamsport, only to find the river swollen and impassable.

On July 6, two divisions of Union cavalry under Gen. John Buford attacked the trapped wagon train. A makeshift force of cavalry, stragglers and wounded Confederates under Gen. John Imboden waged a three-hour battle in extremely adverse conditions before driving off the Union attackers. Arriving with his full force, Lee erected a defensive line around Williamsport, waiting for the river to subside so his engineers could build a pontoon bridge at nearby Falling Waters. For 10 days, the town became a massive hospital for wounded and dying soldiers as a growing Union force amassed for an attack that could have ended the war. Lee was finally able to move his army across the river during the night of July 13. Union cavalry under Gen. George Custer attacked the Confederate rearguard at Falling Waters, inflicting heavy losses. It would be the last fighting of the Gettysburg campaign, with over 1,700 Union and Confederate casualties in the various actions around Williamsport.

Located a mile west of I-81, Williamsport is a classic nineteenth-century Chesapeake and Ohio Canal town. It offers a picturesque town center with quaint shops and eateries. The Town Museum is located in an eighteenth-century barn and showcases Civil War artifacts. While the museum is only open on Sundays, brochures and interpretive markers allow visitors to guide themselves around the town and the important Civil War sites.

The Chesapeake and Ohio Canal National Historical Park is also worth visiting. It is open daily and contains miles of scenic hiking and biking trails.

HOURS
The Town Museum at historic Springfield Farm in Williamsport is open on Sundays from 1 to 4 p.m. between March and October. The Chesapeake and Ohio Canal National Historic Park is open during daylight hours daily except on federal holidays.

INFORMATION
www.williamsportmd.gov/visitors/springfield-farm

www.nps.gov/choh

4. South Mountain, Maryland

The first major battle to take place on Union soil was fought on September 14, 1862, as Union and Confederate forces fought for possession of mountain passes on South Mountain, part of the Blue Ridge Mountains. Learning that Lee was moving his Confederate army toward Hagerstown on the western side of the mountains, McClellan tried to force his army through three mountain passes to cut off Lee's advance. He sent Gen. William Franklin with a force of 12,000 men to capture Crampton's Gap to the south and two corps under Burnside to take Turner's Gap and Fox's Gap six miles to the north.

Franklin was able to overrun the small force of 500 Confederates thinly deployed across Crampton's Gap, but Burnside confronted stiff resistance from Gen. D.H. Hill and 5,000 Confederates defending the two northern passes. Intense fighting continued throughout the day and drew increasing numbers of both armies into the battle. Unable to dislodge Hill's force, Burnside attempted a flanking movement at Frostown Gap that the Confederates stubbornly resisted but were unable to stop. The timely arrival of reinforcements saved the outnumbered Confederates until nightfall, when they were forced to withdraw. Union dead, wounded and missing at the four passes exceeded 2,500, while Confederate casualties were almost 3,800.

Portions of the site of this sprawling engagement are preserved on parts of three Maryland state parks, two National Historic Districts, land preserved by the Civil War Trust and sections of the Appalachian Trail. The nonprofit Friends of the South Mountain Battlefield provides a 22.6-mile driving tour linking the most important areas of the battlefield, with 17 instructional markers and monuments. Visitors are encouraged to begin the tour at Washington Monument State Park, located 17 miles south of Hagerstown off Route 40. The Park features a 15-foot stone column, built in 1827 by local residents as the nation's first monument to George Washington, and a small museum with artifacts from the battle.

The driving tour ends in Gathland State Park, which features a museum located in historic buildings built by George Townsend, a noted Civil War journalist, and a 50-foot high stone arch built in 1896 as a memorial for Civil War correspondents. The area abounds with outdoor hiking trails, panoramic vistas, camping areas and many recreational sites around scenic Greenbrier Lake.

HOURS
South Mountain State Battlefield is open daily from 8 a.m. to sunset. Gathland State Park is open from 8 a.m. to sunset

INFORMATION
www.dnr.maryland.gov/publiclands/pages/western/south-mountainbattlefield.aspx

www.dnr.maryland.gov/publiclands/pages/western/gathland.aspx

5. Wrightsville, Pennsylvania

After invading Pennsylvania in late June 1863, Lee sent part of his army under Lt. Gen. Richard Ewell to capture the state capital of Harrisburg, which was an important transportation point for Union troops heading south. Ewell divided his force, sending Gen. Early to capture York and then cross the Susquehanna River to attack Harrisburg from the east. Early occupied York with little opposition and sent a force under Gen. John B. Gordon east to Wrightsville to secure the mile-long covered bridge across the river. Gordon opened fire with artillery on the entrenched Lancaster County militiamen defending the bridge, who set fire to the bridge as they retreated across the river. Accelerated by high winds, the fire quickly spread over the entire bridge and into nearby sections of Wrightsville. Gordon's Confederates organized bucket brigades with the local townspeople and were able to save much of the town, but not the bridge, which had been the world's longest covered bridge. Had the Confederates been able to secure the bridge and separate themselves from the pursuing Union troops, the Battle of Gettysburg might never have been fought because the war would have moved farther east.

The Wrightsville Historical Museum, located in an 1871 Victorian house, provides exhibits, a library and small gift shop that highlight the story of the building and burning of the Wrightsville-Columbia Bridge as well as other local history. A separate Civil War diorama built by local volunteers offers a light and sound display of the burning of the bridge and the unique cooperation between Confederates and Northern townspeople to save the town.

→ A larger Historical Society Museum and Library (www.yorkhistorycenter.org/york-pa-museums) located in nearby York offers a visitor center, gift shop and Civil War exhibit that highlight the occupation of York and other Civil War events in the area. The museum is open year round, and admission to the museum gives access to other historical sites, such as a restored eighteenth-century colonial village and the historic courthouse that served as the nation's capital in 1778 while the Second Continental Congress met at York.

→ The National Civil War Museum (www.nationalcivilwarmuseum.org) in nearby Harrisburg is the nation's largest museum dedicated solely to the Civil War. The museum is open daily, except Thanksgiving, Christmas, New Year's Day, and Easter.

i

HOURS
The Historic Wrightsville Museum and the Burning of the Bridge Diorama are open Sundays 1 to 4 p.m. or by appointment (call the museum at 717-252-1169).

INFORMATION
www.historicwrightsvillepa.org

6. Chambersburg, Pennsylvania

Following the battle of Antietam, Lee ordered Gen. J.E.B. Stuart to strike into Pennsylvania to capture supplies, disrupt communications lines and create a diversion that might prevent McClellan from launching a counterattack into Virginia. Chambersburg was a thriving market town, county seat and Union supply depot when Stuart encircled the town in October 1862, demanded its surrender, and made off with whatever supplies his men could carry.

Chambersburg would reappear on the Civil War stage. In late June of the following year, Lee occupied the town while supplying his army. Hearing that a large Union force was in pursuit, Lee made the decision to join his scattered army 24 miles to the east — near Gettysburg.

On July 30, 1864, Confederate troops returned to Chambersburg yet again, ordering the residents to pay a ransom and then setting fire to the town in retaliation for homes being burnt in Virginia. With the town's center leveled and some 500 buildings burned, Chambersburg became the only town north of the Mason-Dixon Line to be completely destroyed during the war.

HOURS
The Chambersburg Heritage Center is open Monday through Friday from 8 a.m. to 5 p.m.; from May to late October, the center is open on Saturdays from 10 a.m. to 3 p.m.

INFORMATION
www.chambersburg.org/HeritageCenter

The Chambersburg Heritage Center is located in a marble bank building on the corner of scenic Memorial Square at the center of the town's National Historic District. The Heritage Center offers exhibits telling the story of Chambersburg's role in the war and its earlier history as a frontier outpost and transportation center. A Civil War walking trail begins in Memorial Square and follows trail markers to historic sites throughout the town.

Located a mile west of I-81, Chambersburg is also a showcase of late Victorian architecture, as the various contractors brought in to rebuild the downtown area sought to put their distinctive decorative signature on their buildings. Many cafes, specialty stores, boutiques and antique shops add to the town's unique charm.

7. Carlisle, Pennsylvania

CUMBERLAND VALLEY VISITORS BUREAU

As the Army of Northern Virginia moved northward through Maryland in June 1863, on its way to what would become the defining battle of the war, Gen. Lee divided his force. He sent Ewell's corps toward Carlisle, Pennsylvania, with the aim of moving east to capture the state capital at Harrisburg. At the time Ewell's troops occupied Carlisle on June 27, it was already a sizeable town with a courthouse, college, Union supply depot and military post — the Carlisle Barracks, which housed the U.S. Army Cavalry School. For two days, some 12,000 Confederates occupied the town and raised a Confederate flag over the Carlisle Barracks, making it the northernmost Union installation captured by the Confederates during the war.

A Union force under Gen. W.F. Smith reoccupied the city and was confronted on July 1 by Gen. Stewart and a force of Confederate troops. Stewart bombarded the town for several hours in preparation for an attack when, hearing that Lee was engaged in fighting at Gettysburg, he ordered the barracks and depot burned and withdrew his forces. While producing few casualties, historians consider the engagement significant for isolating a Union division from the broader fighting and, more important, delaying Stewart an entire day, thus depriving Lee of his most trusted source of intelligence.

Located west of the junction of I-81 and the Pennsylvania Turnpike, Carlisle offers numerous museums and historical sites that provide exhibits and tours relating to the Gettysburg campaign and local and military history. A visit should begin with the Cumberland County Historical Society Museum and Library, located in the town's historic district. A visitor center in the museum shop offers guides for walking and driving tours of the area. The Carlisle Barracks, which today houses the Army War College and remnants of the historic Carlisle Indian Industrial School, is open for weekday self-guided tours. The nearby Army Heritage and Education Center offers indoor and walking tour exhibits relating to the Civil War and other eras of Army history. Carlisle's historic district includes most of the original 1751 town plan, with the 1846 courthouse, the historic Carlisle House Inn, Davidson College and over a thousand architecturally significant churches and commercial and residential buildings. With numerous boutiques, antique shops, quaint cafes, an historic theater and art galleries, Carlisle offers a unique blend of historical, military and cultural experiences.

HOURS
The Cumberland County Historical Society Museum and Library are open Tuesday through Friday from 10 a.m. to 4 p.m. and Saturday from 10 a.m. to 2 p.m. The Army Heritage and Education Center is open daily.

INFORMATION
www.historicalsociety.com

ahec.armywarcollege.edu

VEZZANI PHOTOGRAPHY / SHUTTERSTOCK.COM

8. Harpers Ferry, West Virginia

Situated at the confluence of the Potomac and Shenandoah Rivers and in a position to control a vital railway bridge and a canal, Harpers Ferry was an important strategic objective when Lee made plans for his first invasion of the North in September 1862. He wanted to capture the sizeable garrison protecting the town and seize its supplies and ammunition. Lee ordered part of his army under Gen. Thomas "Stonewall" Jackson to attack the town. Two Confederate brigades were able to push defenders from Maryland Heights, overlooking the town. Jackson proceeded to place more than 50 guns on Maryland Heights and nearby Loudoun Heights, on the Virginia side of the Potomac. On September 15, Jackson commenced an artillery barrage from all sides of the town. Realizing the Union position was hopeless, Col. Dixon Miles agreed to surrender the town and turn over 12,000 Union soldiers as prisoners. It would be the largest surrender of Union troops during the war.

Harpers Ferry played a similar role in Gen. Early's plan to launch the third and last Confederate invasion into Maryland in July 1864. Early hoped to neutralize a Union force at Harpers Ferry, secure needed provisions and destroy the railroad bridge to prevent movement of reinforcements from the west. Unlike 1862, the Confederate force that approached the town on July 4 found it abandoned and its defenders in strong positions on Maryland Heights. Recognizing the impossibility of occupying the town without coming under intense enemy artillery fire, Early moved his troops across the Potomac to attack Maryland Heights from the rear. After two days of skirmishing failed to dislodge the Federals, he ordered his force to disengage and proceed east toward Frederick.

The town of Harpers Ferry has been preserved within the Harpers Ferry National Historical Park, a multilayered historical experience that highlights the town's role in the Civil War and also its history in manufacturing, railroads, the Lewis and Clark expedition and, of course, John Brown's famous 1859 raid on the U.S. Armory. The park, which is located 25 miles west of Frederick on Route 340, includes the strategic Maryland and Loudoun Heights which offer panoramic views of the town and surrounding Blue Ridge Mountains.

Visitors can walk the picturesque streets of the restored nineteenth-century industrial town, visit museums and exhibits, participate in ranger-led discussions and tours, hike battlefields and scenic trails and learn about historic Storer College, operated by the Freedman's Bureau to aid and educate African Americans after the war. Along with its many historical and cultural resources, Harpers Ferry offers a variety of family and recreational activities such as ghost tours, a museum, camping, canoeing and whitewater rafting. G

HOURS
Harpers Ferry National Historical Park is open daily from 9 a.m. to 5 p.m. except Thanksgiving, Christmas and New Year's Day.

INFORMATION
www.nps.gov/hafe

The Reconciliation Reunion

Veterans from the North and South came together 100 years ago.

By Mark Greenbaum
Photos from the Library of Congress

The fiftieth anniversary of the Battle of Gettysburg created one of the most extraordinary events in American history. Over 50,000 veterans made their way to Pennsylvania for what would be the largest Civil War reunion. The pictures and accounts of the event remain captivating a century later, and speak to a healing that was unthinkable in 1863.

"The Sores of the War"

Broad reconciliation had been painstaking. Prideful Southerners seethed at the imposition of emancipationist policies and carpetbagger politicians. As Pulitzer Prize–winning historian Paul Buck noted, Reconstruction "went so far as to create a situation of almost permanent sentimental disaffection on the part of the Southerners." It's no surprise then that early Northern attempts at reunion were rebuffed. Many Northerners also remained bitter, firm in the belief that the rebellious Southern states bore sole responsibility for the destruction of the war.

Veterans on each side began forming numerous organizations after 1865, the largest being the Grand Army of the Republic and the United Confederate Veterans, but the two sides rarely met. The first attempt to put together a Gettysburg reunion in 1869 failed, and one in 1874 attracted virtually no Southerners. Invited in 1869, Robert E. Lee rejected the entreaty, calling it "wiser...not to keep open the sores of the war."

A critical change came about because of the disputed presidential election between Rutherford B. Hayes and Samuel Tilden. The Compromise of 1877 installed the Republican Hayes in the White House; in exchange, Northern states relinquished control of states in the South. This allowed Southern enmities to gradually wither. At the same time, there was "a tremendous reversal of opinion," as Buck put it, in Northerners' views of the South.

In the ensuing years, reunions between Union and Confederate veterans became commonplace, including ones at Fredericksburg, Chancellorsville and Kennesaw Mountain. Writing in *The Century* magazine, one writer estimated that 24 reunions between the two sides were held between 1875 and 1879. Large-scale reunions were held in Chicago and at Chickamauga in 1895, with numerous smaller ceremonies occurring at Gettysburg before 1900 as well.

Gatherings at Gettysburg

But Gettysburg was always different. The battle quickly assumed a mythical place in the national consciousness. Americans understood it as the turning point in the war, one that occurred on Northern soil and was decided on the anniversary of the nation's birth.

Beginning in the 1870s, Gettysburg had been the site of regular reunions of Pennsylvania veterans. It became a mecca for war remembrance and the de facto location for states seeking to honor their fallen. By the 1880s the battlefield would hold more than 300 markers, becoming in the words of the *Gettysburg Compiler*, a "forest of marble and granite, iron and bronze."

An 1887 reunion brought 500 Pennsylvania veterans and 200 from Virginia. Speaking there, CSA Col. William Aylet extolled the creation of "a new empire" from "the ashes left by war." At ceremonies the next year, Union Gen. Daniel Sickles, who lost his right leg at Gettysburg, proclaimed "today there are no victors, no vanquished" on "the America born on this battlefield." These warm feelings carried into the new century, perhaps best captured by a newspaper which editorialized, "the past is dead...let us live in the present." Speaking at a reunion in New Orleans in 1909, President William Howard Taft emphasized the importance of "fraternization and forgetfulness."

As Gettysburg's 50th anniversary approached, Gen. H.S. Huidekoper successfully lobbied Pennsylvania Gov. Edwin Stuart to hold a celebration. Coordinating with Congress, the other states, and veterans groups, a commission planned for a four-day event. Congress agreed to build a camp, and the states consented to cover most travel costs for their veterans. The United States Army built more than 6,500 tents, separated by state over a 280-acre plot and supported by newly installed water and sewage systems, six hospital facilities and even a post office. About 2,000 cooks and laborers would prepare nearly 700,000 meals. Approximately 1,500 troops patrolled the camp and its elderly charges, who were attended by a fleet of attendants and boys from the newly formed Boy Scouts.

An Unprecedented Event

Approximately 45,000 Union veterans and 8,700 Confederates arrived for the event in 1913. They ranged in age from 61-year-old John Lincoln Clem

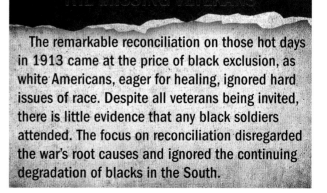

THE MISSING VETERANS

The remarkable reconciliation on those hot days in 1913 came at the price of black exclusion, as white Americans, eager for healing, ignored hard issues of race. Despite all veterans being invited, there is little evidence that any black soldiers attended. The focus on reconciliation disregarded the war's root causes and ignored the continuing degradation of blacks in the South.

> *"We have found one another again as brothers and comrades in arms, enemies no longer, generous friends rather, our battles long past..."*

(see sidebar to the right) to Micyah Weiss, purportedly 112. Despite blistering heat that topped over 100 degrees, only nine veterans died, speaking to heartiness of the survivors, who, as pictures attest, rarely took off their heavy coats. Men mingled amicably, swapping anecdotes and stories.

There were many memorable exchanges. At Cemetery Ridge, several groups of veterans converged to survey the Angle. One Confederate veteran, A.C. Smith of the 56th Virginia, pointed to the exact spot where he had been wounded, movingly noting that he would have died had a Union soldier not saved his life. At that moment, a nearby blue, Albert Hamilton of the 72nd Pennsylvania, perked up and approached Smith, and described how he had watered a wounded rebel during the battle and then carried him to a field hospital. Stunned, Smith grabbed Hamilton and stared at him for a long moment before exclaiming, "You are the man."

Perhaps the most emotional part of the week was a reenactment of Pickett's Charge, as veterans converged at the Angle to embrace. Over the week, the men were treated to a fireworks display over Little Round Top and a progression of speakers, including governors, congressmen and various dignitaries, topped by an address from President Woodrow Wilson on July 4.

For the most part, Wilson's speech mirrored those of every other speaker, emphasizing the valor of the veterans and the sacrifice of the fallen while saying nothing of the causes of the war: "We have found one another again as brothers and comrades in arms, enemies no longer, generous friends rather, our battles long past, the quarrel forgotten — except that we shall not forget the splendid valor."

The reunion was almost universally praised as a triumph that completed the healing of the nation. The *San Francisco Chronicle* wrote, "there has been nothing like it in the history of mankind," while the *Philadelphia Inquirer* opined that with the reunion closed, "the final test has been made; the verdict has been accepted by all." **G**

THE CHILD SERGEANT

The youngest veteran at the reunion was John Lincoln Clem. Running away from home in 1861, he attempted to enlist in the Union Army but was rejected due to his age: He was all of 10 years old. Undeterred, he tagged along with the 22nd Michigan. The soldiers adopted him as their mascot and the officers chipped in to pay him $13 a month. He was eventually allowed to enlist in 1863.

Clem became a national celebrity after he fought, using a sawed-off musket, at Chickamauga in 1863. A Confederate spotted Clem and said, according to legend, either "I think the best thing a mite of a chap like you can do is drop that gun" or "damned little Yankee devil." Clem proceeded to shoot the Confederate, earning a promotion to sergeant.

Clem rejoined the military in 1870 and served until 1915. He died in 1937 at the age of 85.

John Clem in 1863 and at Gettysburg in 1913 (inset).

CIVIL WAR TIMELINE

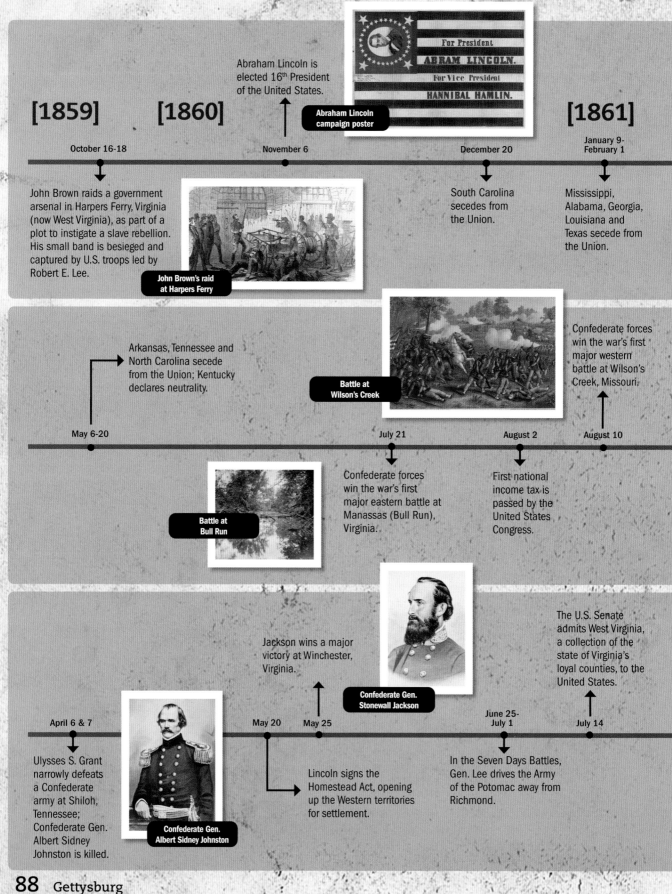

[1859]

October 16-18

John Brown raids a government arsenal in Harpers Ferry, Virginia (now West Virginia), as part of a plot to instigate a slave rebellion. His small band is besieged and captured by U.S. troops led by Robert E. Lee.

John Brown's raid at Harpers Ferry

[1860]

November 6

Abraham Lincoln is elected 16th President of the United States.

For President ABRAM LINCOLN.
For Vice President HANNIBAL HAMLIN.

Abraham Lincoln campaign poster

December 20

South Carolina secedes from the Union.

[1861]

January 9-February 1

Mississippi, Alabama, Georgia, Louisiana and Texas secede from the Union.

May 6-20

Arkansas, Tennessee and North Carolina secede from the Union; Kentucky declares neutrality.

July 21

Confederate forces win the war's first major eastern battle at Manassas (Bull Run), Virginia.

Battle at Bull Run

Battle at Wilson's Creek

August 2

First national income tax is passed by the United States Congress.

August 10

Confederate forces win the war's first major western battle at Wilson's Creek, Missouri.

April 6 & 7

Ulysses S. Grant narrowly defeats a Confederate army at Shiloh, Tennessee; Confederate Gen. Albert Sidney Johnston is killed.

Confederate Gen. Albert Sidney Johnston

May 20

Lincoln signs the Homestead Act, opening up the Western territories for settlement.

May 25

Jackson wins a major victory at Winchester, Virginia.

Confederate Gen. Stonewall Jackson

June 25-July 1

In the Seven Days Battles, Gen. Lee drives the Army of the Potomac away from Richmond.

July 14

The U.S. Senate admits West Virginia, a collection of the state of Virginia's loyal counties, to the United States.

Fort Sumter, a small federal base in the harbor of Charleston, South Carolina, is bombarded by Confederate batteries after Lincoln orders its garrison to be resupplied.

Fort Sumter

February 8-9

The Confederate States of America establish a provisional government and elect Jefferson Davis as president.

Confederate President Jefferson Davis

April 12-13

April 17

Virginia secedes from the Union.

April 19

President Lincoln declares a blockade of ports from South Carolina to Texas.

May 3

Lincoln calls for 75,000 volunteer soldiers.

Battle at Pea Ridge

Confederate Gen. Stonewall Jackson suffers his only battlefield loss, at Kernstown, Virginia; the Union Army diverts reinforcements from the Virginia Peninsula to contend with Jackson in the Shenandoah Valley.

[1862]

Union forces win a surprise victory at Pea Ridge, Arkansas.

March 7 & 8 **March 8 & 9**

March 17

March 23

The Battle of Hampton Roads, Virginia, pits two ironclad warships against each other for the first time in world history; they fight to a stalemate.

The Union Army of the Potomac, led by George McClellan, lands on the Virginia Peninsula with the intention of advancing and capturing Richmond.

Battle of the Monitor and the Merrimac

Union Gen. George McClellan

The Confederate invasion of the Northeast is halted with the Battle of Antietam (Sharpsburg), Maryland; 23,000 casualties are suffered, more lives lost and damaged than in any other single day in American history.

The Confederacy drives back a Union offensive at the Battle of Fredericksburg, Virginia.

McClellan at the Battle of Antietam

August 28-30

September 17

October 8

December 7

December 13-15

Lee's Army of Northern Virginia defeats a Union army at the Second Battle of Manassas (Bull Run) Virginia; Lee begins to plan an invasion of the Northeast.

The Confederate invasion of Kentucky is repulsed at the Battle of Perryville.

Union forces solidify their hold on northwest Arkansas after winning the Battle of Prairie Grove.

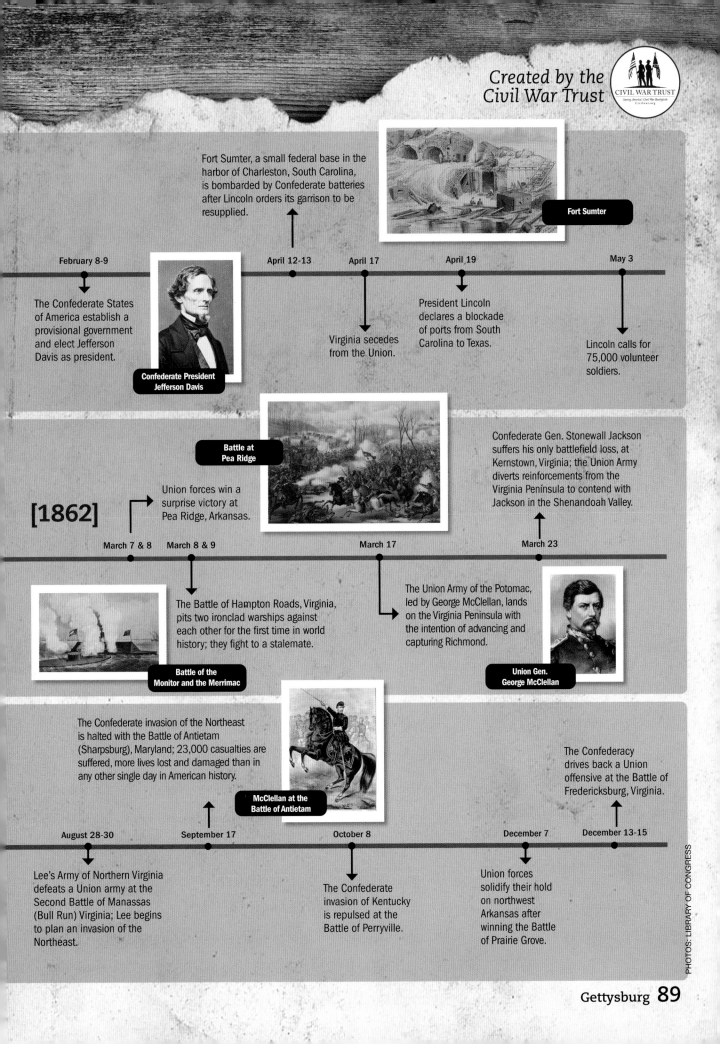

CIVIL WAR TIMELINE

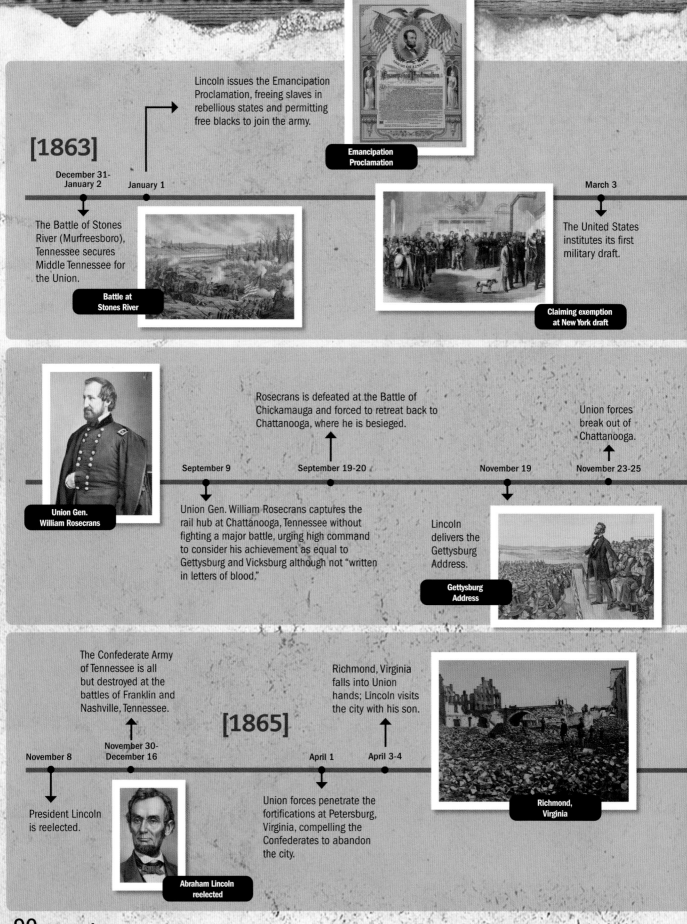

Emancipation Proclamation

Lincoln issues the Emancipation Proclamation, freeing slaves in rebellious states and permitting free blacks to join the army.

[1863]

December 31-
January 2

January 1

The Battle of Stones River (Murfreesboro), Tennessee secures Middle Tennessee for the Union.

Battle at Stones River

March 3

The United States institutes its first military draft.

Claiming exemption at New York draft

Union Gen. William Rosecrans

September 9

Union Gen. William Rosecrans captures the rail hub at Chattanooga, Tennessee without fighting a major battle, urging high command to consider his achievement as equal to Gettysburg and Vicksburg although not "written in letters of blood."

September 19-20

Rosecrans is defeated at the Battle of Chickamauga and forced to retreat back to Chattanooga, where he is besieged.

November 19

Lincoln delivers the Gettysburg Address.

Gettysburg Address

November 23-25

Union forces break out of Chattanooga.

[1865]

The Confederate Army of Tennessee is all but destroyed at the battles of Franklin and Nashville, Tennessee.

November 8

President Lincoln is reelected.

November 30-
December 16

Abraham Lincoln reelected

April 1

Union forces penetrate the fortifications at Petersburg, Virginia, compelling the Confederates to abandon the city.

April 3-4

Richmond, Virginia falls into Union hands; Lincoln visits the city with his son.

Richmond, Virginia

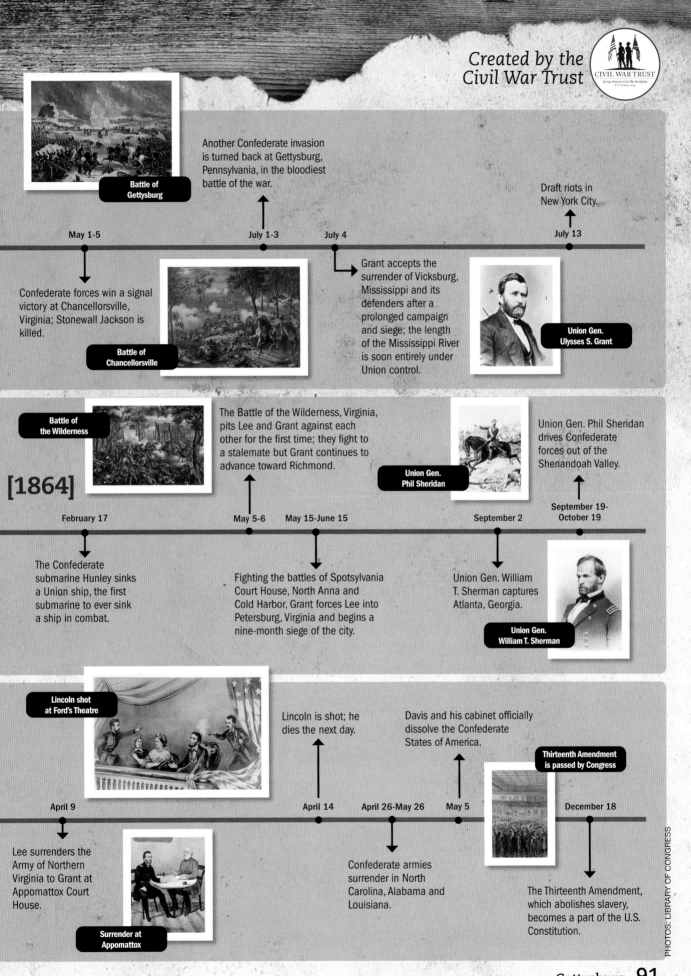

Created by the Civil War Trust

CIVIL WAR TRUST
Saving America's Civil War Battlefields
Civilwar.org

Battle of Gettysburg

Another Confederate invasion is turned back at Gettysburg, Pennsylvania, in the bloodiest battle of the war.

Draft riots in New York City.

May 1-5   July 1-3   July 4   July 13

Confederate forces win a signal victory at Chancellorsville, Virginia; Stonewall Jackson is killed.

Grant accepts the surrender of Vicksburg, Mississippi and its defenders after a prolonged campaign and siege; the length of the Mississippi River is soon entirely under Union control.

Battle of Chancellorsville

Union Gen. Ulysses S. Grant

Battle of the Wilderness

The Battle of the Wilderness, Virginia, pits Lee and Grant against each other for the first time; they fight to a stalemate but Grant continues to advance toward Richmond.

Union Gen. Phil Sheridan drives Confederate forces out of the Shenandoah Valley.

Union Gen. Phil Sheridan

[1864]

February 17   May 5-6   May 15-June 15   September 2   September 19-October 19

The Confederate submarine Hunley sinks a Union ship, the first submarine to ever sink a ship in combat.

Fighting the battles of Spotsylvania Court House, North Anna and Cold Harbor, Grant forces Lee into Petersburg, Virginia and begins a nine-month siege of the city.

Union Gen. William T. Sherman captures Atlanta, Georgia.

Union Gen. William T. Sherman

Lincoln shot at Ford's Theatre

Lincoln is shot; he dies the next day.

Davis and his cabinet officially dissolve the Confederate States of America.

Thirteenth Amendment is passed by Congress

April 9   April 14   April 26-May 26   May 5   December 18

Lee surrenders the Army of Northern Virginia to Grant at Appomattox Court House.

Confederate armies surrender in North Carolina, Alabama and Louisiana.

The Thirteenth Amendment, which abolishes slavery, becomes a part of the U.S. Constitution.

Surrender at Appomattox

PHOTOS: LIBRARY OF CONGRESS

A great deal is known about the Civil War. Armies of amateur and professional historians have dissected it in sometimes astonishing detail. But definitive statistics and analysis remain elusive. For example, a recent paper estimated that the true fatality count of the Civil War could be as high as 850,000. The generally accepted figure of 620,000 fatalities was first put forward by William F. Fox and Thomas Leonard Livermore in 1889; Union veterans, they meticulously combed documentation such as pension records. However, their list would have missed, for example, a civilian who died of an illness contracted at an Army camp, and much of their work on the Confederate toll amounted to educated guesses.

Historians are constantly amending and correcting our view of the war, but the picture will never be totally clear: Too many accounts are contradictory, too much documentation is missing, and, of course, too much time has gone by. But the big picture is clear: The Civil War was a war without equal.

THE MILITARY POPULATION

Roughly 2.1 million men fought for the Union and 1.1 men fought for the Confederacy. The mortality rate for these soldiers was remarkably high, especially compared to our recent wars.

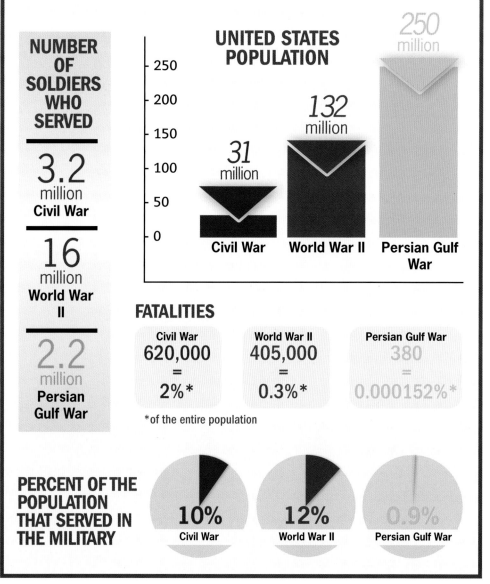

NUMBER OF SOLDIERS WHO SERVED

3.2 million — Civil War

16 million — World War II

2.2 million — Persian Gulf War

UNITED STATES POPULATION

- Civil War — 31 million
- World War II — 132 million
- Persian Gulf War — 250 million

FATALITIES

Civil War	World War II	Persian Gulf War
620,000	405,000	380
=	=	=
2%*	0.3%*	0.000152%*

*of the entire population

PERCENT OF THE POPULATION THAT SERVED IN THE MILITARY

- 10% Civil War
- 12% World War II
- 0.9% Persian Gulf War

WAGES OF WAR

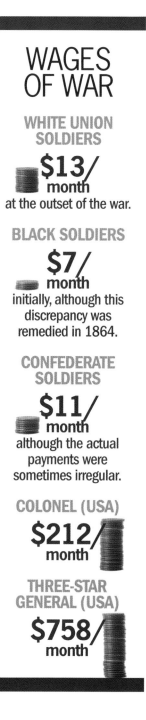

WHITE UNION SOLDIERS
$13/month
at the outset of the war.

BLACK SOLDIERS
$7/month
initially, although this discrepancy was remedied in 1864.

CONFEDERATE SOLDIERS
$11/month
although the actual payments were sometimes irregular.

COLONEL (USA)
$212/month

THREE-STAR GENERAL (USA)
$758/month

BLOODIEST BATTLES

Gettysburg stands out as the bloodiest battle of the Civil War. The battle's second day, in which about 20,000 men became casualties, would rank as the tenth bloodiest battle of the war by itself.

Gettysburg 51,000	Shiloh 23,746
Chickamauga 34,624	Stones River 23,515
Spotsylvania 30,000	Antietam 22,717
The Wilderness 29,800	Second Manassas 22,180
Chancellorsville 24,000	Vicksburg 19,233

THE AVERAGE SOLDIER

THE AVERAGE AGE

25.8 years old

Most soldiers were between the ages of 18 and 45. Slightly less than half of the Union soldiers and slightly more than half of the Confederate soldiers had been farmers before the war.

THE AVERAGE HEIGHT	THE AVERAGE WEIGHT
5 ft. 8.25 in.	143.5 lbs.

Many soldiers on both sides, particularly the North, were foreign born. Up to a quarter of the Union Army may have been immigrants.

Germans (largest group)	→ Irish	→ Canadians	→ English

1863
the year AfricanAmericans were allowed to enlist.

180,000
number of men in the U.S. Colored Troops by the end of the war.

ARMY ORGANIZATION

Companies
→ Companies were lettered in alphabetical order (with the letter J omitted because it was too similar in appearance to I).
→ Led by captains.

Approximately **100** men*

Regiments
→ Comprised of 10 companies, regiments were the fundamental military unit.
→ Led by lieutenant colonels or colonels.

Approximately **1,000***

Brigades
→ Comprised of 4 to 6 regiments, brigades were the tactical infantry units.
→ Led by colonels or brigadier generals.

Approximately **4,000-6,000***

Divisions
→ Comprised of 2 to 4 brigades, divisions were the basic unit of operational maneuver on the battlefield. Confederate divisions tended to be slightly larger than Union divisions.
→ Commanded by brigadier or major general on the Union side and by major generals on the Confederate side.

Approximately **8,000-24,000***

Corps
→ Comprised of 2+ divisions, corps were the largest military unit and were small armies unto themselves.
→ Led by major generals on the Union side and lieutenant generals for the Confederacy.
→ Union corps were designated by number I-XXV.
→ Confederate corps were designated by numbers duplicated in the East and West, but were usually referred to by their commanding officer's name (ex. Jackson's Corps instead of II Corps in the East).

Approximately **16,000-48,000***

* These numbers reflect the theoretical strength of a full-sized unit; the actual fighting strength was typically much smaller.

Sources: Civil War Trust; NPS.gov; WW II Memorial; The Civil War Dictionary; Regimental Losses in the American Civil War, 1861-1865

A Union in Peril

The map to the right was published in 1856 by William Reynolds, a supporter of the newly formed Republican party. In the upper left is John Fremont, the Republican presidential candidate; the upper right shows William Dayton, the Republican candidate for vice president.

Four slave states (shown on the map as dark gray) did not secede:

• The DELAWARE legislature voted overwhelmingly against secession; the state had limited slavery and deep ties to the North.

• Although MARYLAND never left the Union, many parts of Maryland were strongly pro-slavery and pro-South and contributed troops to the Confederacy. In the Battle of Front Royal, the 1st Maryland (Confederate States of America) and 1st Maryland (United States) famously fought against each other. When the Southerners won and took prisoners, "nearly all recognized old friends and acquaintances, whom they greeted cordially," according to Charles Goldsborough, who was taken prisoner by his brother, William.

• KENTUCKY declared neutrality at the start of the war, but gradually shifted to support of the Union. Many Kentuckians still supported the South; a provisional pro-South government was erected and Kentucky, although a Union state, was also admitted to the Confederate States of America.

• MISSOURI, like Kentucky, stayed in the Union but was also recognized by the Confederacy as a member state. Missouri was the site of recurring guerilla warfare.

• In addition, pro-North WEST VIRGINIA broke off from Virginia in 1862.

This illustration depicts the Baltimore Riot of 1861, when pro-Confederacy Marylanders attacked Union soldiers en route to Washington, D.C. Sixteen people died in the melee — the first bloodshed of the Civil War.

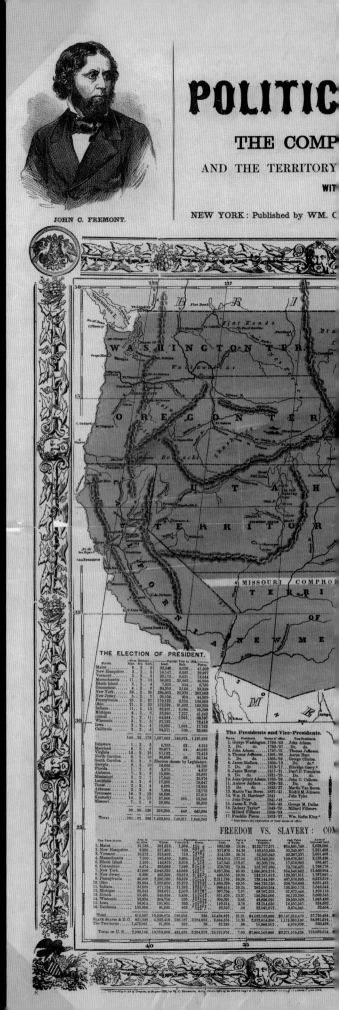

JOHN C. FREMONT.

POLITIC

THE COMP

AND THE TERRITORY

WIT

NEW YORK : Published by WM. C

THE ELECTION OF PRESIDENT.

FREEDOM VS. SLAVERY : CO

The Presidents and Vice-Presidents.